PENGUIN BO

WAR JOURNEY

Malaravan, born in April 1972 near Jaffna, was the youngest of his four siblings. He joined the Tamil Eelam movement in 1990.

N. Malathy is a member of the Sri Lankan Tamil diaspora who has lived in New Zealand for four decades. She is a computer scientist who has engaged with and written extensively on the human rights situation in Sri Lanka.

WAR JOURNEY

Diary of a Tamil Tiger

MALARAVAN

Translated from the Tamil by
N. MALATHY

PENGUIN BOOKS
An imprint of Penguin Random House

PENGUIN BOOKS

USA | Canada | UK | Ireland | Australia
New Zealand | India | South Africa | China

Penguin Books is part of the Penguin Random House group of companies
whose addresses can be found at global.penguinrandomhouse.com

Published by Penguin Random House India Pvt. Ltd
7th Floor, Infinity Tower C, DLF Cyber City,
Gurgaon 122 002, Haryana, India

 Penguin
Random House
India

First published in Tamil in Sri Lanka as *Por Ulaa* by LTTE Publication
Division 1993
Reprinted in Tamil in the United Kingdom as *Por Ulaa* by LTTE International
Secretariat 1994
First published in Tamil in India as *Por Ulaa* by Vidiyal Pathippagam,
Coimbatore 2009
First published by Penguin Books India 2013

ISBN 9780143417361

Typeset in Sabon MT by Eleven Arts, Delhi
Printed at Repro India Limited

www.penguin.co.in

For the maaveerar of Tamil Eelam

Contents

Contents

Meeting Malaravan
Translator's Note

This is the translation of a book written in 1990 by Malaravan, a member of the Liberation Tigers of Tamil Eelam (LTTE). Malaravan is the name given to him by the LTTE. Among his comrades he was also known as Leo. The book is in the form of a travel- and battle-diary. There is a lot of writing attributed to members of the LTTE; Malaravan's writing is unique among them for the breadth and depth of the subject matter he covers.

I did not meet Malaravan in person. He was killed in November 1992 at the age of twenty in the battle lines. He is a 'maaveerar'—a member of the Tamil Eelam armed movement killed in confrontation with the enemy—in Eelam Tamil usage. I met him in 2007 in a library in the town of Kilinochchi in Vanni (an area in northern Sri Lanka) through his book, *Por Ulaa* (War Journey). The manuscript for this book as well as all of Malaravan's other writing was found in his luggage by comrades after his death, and handed over to his seniors. LTTE's publication division brought out *Por Ulaa* in 1993, and it won the prize for the best Tamil book published in the island that year. In the same library I also came to know of many other maaveerar writers, besides living writers (LTTE members), through their writings. I was volunteering at the time in Vanni, following an internationally-sanctioned ceasefire in 2002. Vanni was under the LTTE and remained so until its defeat in 2009.

A member of the Eelam Tamil diaspora, I had lived in New Zealand, away from the Tamil homeland, for many decades. I went back excited by the Norwegian-sponsored ceasefire and the peace process. While in Vanni, from 2005 to 2009, I worked for the human rights body, the North East Secretariat on Human Rights (NESoHR), helped the LTTE Peace Secretariat write reports for submission at the Geneva peace talks in 2006, and worked with UNICEF and the LTTE to end child recruitment[1].

By the year 2007 the ceasefire had already started to weaken. The Lankan government imposed a strict fuel embargo on Vanni. Now there was severe power shortage. Until then electricity had been supplied using fuel, and was managed under the LTTE administrative system. The enforced outages meant I had time on my hands. I began looking for things to do. This took me to the library where I met Malaravan. I did all the translation work for this book using paper and pencil rather than a laptop or computer because electricity was a precious resource that had to be used for other purposes.

When I began my library visits I had no intention of doing any translations. It was Malaravan's writing that drove me to

[1]My experiences are recorded in a book published in 2012 by Clarity Press, USA, titled: *A Fleeting Moment in My Country: The Last Years of the LTTE De-Facto State.*

it. I was astonished by the skill of someone as young as he in penning this first-hand account that brings to life the social and military scenarios of the nineties. It was much later—after I had finished the first draft of the translation—that I decided to find out more about this young writer. In the process, I not only learnt about the rest of his work, but also gained some knowledge about the literature written by the members of the LTTE.

I was particularly attracted to the works of individual members based on their own experiences. The vast majority of these writers were in their early twenties. Their writings, by and large, consisted of short stories and poetry. Malaravan was among the very few who wrote book-length works. I was impressed by the insights on social ills that their writing provided. These writers differed sharply from the majority of young Tamils who have very little understanding of the fabric of the society in which they live. Harsh as this may sound, it was also the way I grew up; and so did many in my parents' generation, my generation and even in my children's generation. The writers I met in the Kilinochchi library were sensitized to their social surroundings. Through them I saw, first-hand, how a struggle against an oppressive government can gather momentum against so many other social ills, and influence and enlighten passive, self-centred young people. These young people came across to me as an almost different species by the degree of awareness they possessed.

Malaravan was a product of this unique society. What made him stand out even more was his exceptional intelligence and his inherent love for other living things as described in the article by his mother. He was a topper in his studies who had just turned eighteen. Born at a unique juncture in the Tamil Eelam history, his intelligence and loving nature sensitized him to greater things. He became a driven young man.

Though we know him only through his writings today, in his two years and four months as an LTTE member, Malaravan achieved a great deal. He underwent the usual military training given to all new LTTE members. He took part in his first military operation a few months later as the leader of a fifteen-member unit. In this battle in September 1990, the Lankan military which had taken refuge at the Dutch Fort in Jaffna was ousted. From this fort, situated very close to the city centre, the Lankan military had been terrorizing civilians in the surrounding area with random artillery fire. Malaravan took part in another smaller-scale battle before going to Manalaaru where he received further military training. In *Por Ulaa*, Malaravan recorded his journey with his comrades from Manalaaru to the Maankulam battle of November 1990.

Malaravan went on to take part in three more battles. In the Silaavathurai battle in 1991 he was injured and was treated by his brother, a medical doctor. Shrapnel close to Malaravan's kidney had to be removed. Immediately after being treated by his brother, Malaravan returned to the battle lines and remained there until the successful completion of the battle. He went back to Jaffna to recuperate only after that. He also took part in the 1991 battle to capture Elephant Pass, a battle in which the LTTE met with severe losses. However, Malaravan's unit succeeded in destroying the Elephant Pass communication tower of the Lankan military. Malaravan took part in his last battle in his division, the Paseelan Mortar Unit, to defend the bases in Manalaaru against the

Lankan military. With this battle the unit was dissolved for military reasons.

Malaravan was then appointed the coordinator of the student division for Jaffna district. He carried out this duty for eight months until July 1992. His role changed again to that of a military analyst/report writer whose task was to analyse completed battles and the resulting military situation, and draft reports on them. During this time, Tamilselvan, who later became the Head of the Political Division, was the military commander for Jaffna district. Commenting on one of the extensive military reports that Malaravan had drafted, Tamilselvan reportedly said that it would have been an excellent book on military matters. For reasons of military secrecy, however, it was never published. Under Tamilselvan's command, an attack was launched in Jaffna, and Malaravan was with him as his military analyst/reporter. Since the pooralis taking part in the battle had either moved forward or were injured, there was no one around to collect the weapons left by the withdrawing Lankan forces. Malaravan went forward to collect them. While walking back with the weapons he was hit by Lankan artillery fire and seriously injured. He later succumbed to his injuries.

I learnt much about Malaravan's roles in the LTTE from his doctor-brother whom I first met in Kilinochchi only in mid-2008. He was a writer too. Indeed, Malaravan came from a family of writers. His maternal grandfather wrote under the pen name Kachchaayil Raththinam. He was well known among Eelam Tamils for his short stories, novels and plays. Foremost among his works is the novel, *Vanniyin Selvi*. Malaravan's mother is also a writer whose work has been published widely. She wrote under the pen name Malarannai, which is also the name of the publishing house owned by the family.

Por Ulaa describes the battle for Maankulam. Maankulam is situated roughly in the middle of the Vanni area. The LTTE controlled most of Vanni at that time. However, the Lankan military had a strong presence in the area, with the Maankulam camp cutting up the large swathe of land under LTTE control. Eviction of the Lankan military from this camp would thus have brought a much larger contiguous area under the LTTE's control. In that sense, this Maankulam battle was an important milestone towards the formation of a de facto state under the LTTE.

The Lankan military, however, recaptured part of Vanni that was under the LTTE, namely Kilinochchi and the surrounding area, in 1996. It was reclaimed by the LTTE in 1998. The de facto state under them eventually came to an end in 2009. The memoir speaks not only about military matters, but also brings out the relationship between the people and the pooralis. There are many places in the book where Malaravan brings up this relationship very naturally. Once, as Malaravan and his comrades sat by the roadside under a tree, tired and hungry, the village women brought food to them. He describes in this incident the care extended by the women to the tired pooralis. The women mixed the rice and curries and made small balls of the food using their hands and placed them in the hands of each poorali to eat. Such a gesture is traditionally regarded among Tamils as an intimate moment between mother and child, both young and old, which is often recalled with nostalgia by adults.

In another incident, Malaravan and his friends needed a place to wash up after driving all night. They walked into the yard of a small hut and asked for permission to use it. From the description of the hut Malaravan shows that the hut belonged to a poor family. The woman in the house showed them the well and gave them toothpaste. She then gave them all tea inside the house, made with fresh cow's milk.

In one of the most touching scenes involving ordinary folks and the pooralis, Malaravan describes the welcome given by the people to the pooralis who were on the move, continuing the battle. As they were leaving after bidding goodbye to the people they stopped the vehicle because an old lady in a white sari was running towards them. She put sweet rice in the mouth of each poorali and kissed each of them on their cheek. Nothing could demonstrate better the love of the people for the pooralis than this small incident. Malaravan says, 'Our heavy hearts melted at her touch.'

The help offered by menfolk in preparation for the battle is brought out clearly by Malaravan in another instance. He describes how each day, fifty men from a different village came to help in the preparation for the battle—mainly in clearing up and digging trenches. Through his description Malaravan demonstrates the enthusiasm of the menfolk who ignored the noises of firing that could be heard in the background. Among these men Malaravan also finds a retired school teacher. I have heard of similar instances in Vanni during the 2008–09 battles too. Men were persuaded to assist in battle preparations. Unlike the time Malaravan describes (when weapons used by the Sri Lankan military were not as lethal), during the

2008–09 battles, many menfolk who went to the battle lines to assist the pooralis were killed by far more lethal weapons that had much longer reach.

During the translation of the book I also had to learn the detailed geography of the area described in it—one I was not familiar with until then. As I learnt the geography I also made a map of the route that Malaravan and his comrades travelled on, especially for this translated version. A young, female LTTE member helped with the making of the digital map.

Malaravan describes a lot of military matters in the book, of which I am ignorant. It was Marshall alias Ilanthirayan, the LTTE military spokesperson, who explained to me the military matters in this book. He told me about the size and strength of the various ammunitions and how they could be identified by their names, etc.; but due to my inability or disinterest, I have failed to absorb much of what he taught me, though some of it has found its way into the translation. The explanations of military terms was also given to me by Marshall.

Marshall helped me visualize some of the scenarios Malaravan describes. As they went into the Maankulam battle, Malaravan and his friends travelled in a small truck-like vehicle with a heavy box in the back containing their machine gun, around which the comrades would sit. Often, while travelling, they would sit talking on the edge of this open truck, facing each other. I also had trouble visualizing the site of the main attack in the Maankulam battle that Malaravan describes.

The main spot is the tall observation tower of the Sri Lankan military which faced a large open field on one side. Malaravan's comrades had to attack the camp from the other end of this open field thus exposing themselves to great danger: from being detected early and also from the landmines the Sri Lankan military would have placed in the open fields.

At that time I thought to myself that it would be difficult to translate this book living outside Vanni. It was a book set in that social context. Translating it while living with people who had long experienced that social context made much more sense. Indeed, when I travelled the roads in Vanni, I was often reminded of *Por Ulaa* where an incident associated with the section of the road I was travelling on had been described.

After his death, except for *Por Ulaa*, the rest of Malaravan's writings were handed over to his family. He had written a novel, *Puyal Paravay* (Hurricane Bird) after *Por Ulaa*. Just three or four years before he wrote this novel, women had become active within the militant movements in Jaffna. Women had also started to engage in military battles. Malaravan took up this theme—together with the liberation of women in general—in this novel. The genuineness of this work on women's liberation, and that too by a Jaffna lad of twenty, blew me away. I read it only after I had completed the first draft of the translation of *Por Ulaa*. *Puyal Paravay* reaffirmed and enhanced my admiration for Malaravan. Published in 2003, it won the prize for the best Tamil novel published that year in the island.

Following the destruction in Vanni in May 2009, I am still struggling to get a copy of *Puyal Paravay*. Indeed, the loss of literature that Eelam Tamils have faced is immeasurable. The burning of the Jaffna Public Library in 1981 is perhaps the biggest-ever instance of the destruction of invaluable ancient manuscripts and materials in recent history. The mass exodus of people from Jaffna in 1996 also resulted in the loss of a lot of writing. The Indian government has been accused of confiscating such material in the safekeeping of various groups in Tamil Nadu with Eelam sympathies. The destruction wrought in Vanni in May 2009 erased another large collection of written literature. Eelam Tamils are still struggling to recover at least some of the writings lost during these disastrous events.

Malaravan had two more books: collections of poetry. Like *Puyal Paravay*, they were brought out by Malarannai Publications owned by his family. To my knowledge, copies of these two books by Malaravan are also presently not available. The title of one of them, *En Kallarai Meel Thoovunkal* (Sprinkle [flowers] on My Grave—Pay Homage at My Grave), is taken from a poem in the book. The ability to imagine one's own death and speak of it so touchingly at such a tender age is exceptional. I am reminded of another famous writer, Lasantha Wickremasinghe, assassinated in 2009—it is widely said, by Lankan forces—who also wrote an extraordinary obituary for himself.

When Malaravan was killed, as is the practice in the LTTE on losing a member, his leader, Tamilselvan, visited his parents. In his foreword to *Por Ulaa*, Tamilselvan wrote that he was full of trepidation when he went to their home. The family, however, welcomed him. Malaravan's father then handed Tamilselvan a cheque for the full amount in the savings account they had opened for Malaravan's education. Their request was to set up a scholarship fund for poor students. The profits from the Malarannai Publications which brought out other books by Malaravan were also put into this fund.

I have often thought about a Malaravan still living in Vanni when I was there in 2007. He would have been nearly forty years old then. What kind of leader would he have been with the benefit of twenty years' experience since writing those books? If at twenty he had such insight and was capable of inspiring so many, what might he have achieved by forty? It is hard not to mourn such a loss.

When I translated *Por Ulaa* in 2007, I did not for a moment imagine that the society that created Malaravan would be destroyed. At that time I was only hoping to inform the world, through Malaravan's writing, of the nature of the society that created him. Things have changed since I translated the book, but his writing still stands out to inform the world about much that continues to be misrepresented or blacked out.

N. Malathy
2012

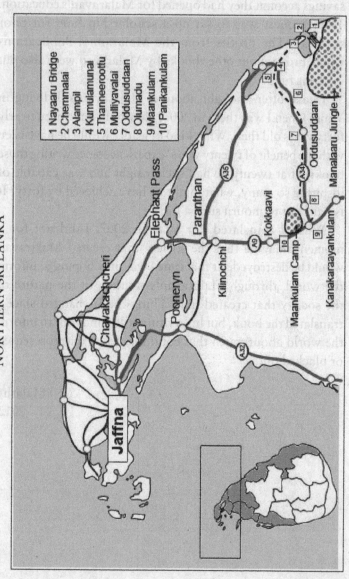

NORTHERN SRI LANKA

1 Nayaaru Bridge
2 Chemmalai
3 Alampil
4 Kumulamunai
5 Thanneerootu
6 Mulliyavalai
7 Oddusuddaan
8 Olumadu
9 Maankulam
10 Panikankulam

Jaffna

Elephant Pass

Paranthan

Chavakacheri

Pooneryn

Kilinochchi

Kokkaavil

Manalaaru Jungle

Oddusuddaan

Kanakaraayankulam

Maankulam Camp

A35

A9

A34

A32

Goodbye Jungle, Goodbye Friend

9 November 1990

The cold November wind whistled. Clouds rushing by cut across the milky light of the moon, but it kept peeping out to smile. Dark clouds gathered at the far end of the eastern sky. Scattered stars twinkled. Occasionally, night birds passed by. An alkaaddi flew past nearby, screaming eerily.

'Appa always says that an alkaaddi's scream is a bad omen. Once when his father was leaving home, an alkaaddi flew by, screaming. My grandmother tried to stop him, but he was too drunk to listen to her. The next day, early in the morning, people from the neighbouring village brought back his body. Apparently somebody had pulled him off his cart and beaten him to death,' Vasanthan said, very seriously.

'Your father has told you this tale, knowing well that you are a fool. If you tell this story to other people they will tease the hell out of you,' said Ithayan.

'Vasanthan is telling *me* this story. Why are you teasing him?' I butted in. Vasanthan took a swipe at Ithayan with the stick he had picked up and only then quietened down.

The tractor trailer in which we were travelling left the open road and started along a forest path. Everyone held their stomachs.

'It will be like driving on a railway track from now on,' laughed Salam, the driver.

'This fellow is a sadist. He deliberately drives recklessly to see us scream in pain,' Vasanthan said, helplessly.

The forest roads were made with tree trunks placed lengthwise. To stop the trunks from being washed away by rain, wooden logs were placed across them and the spaces in between were filled with soil which was then rammed in. Roads built like this must be redone each year after the rainy season is over. This may sound easy, but the work involved is back-breaking. Clearing the forest for the road is a big task in itself. Trees must be chopped into logs and carried to the road. Then the soil must be levelled where mounds have formed and the mud, carried away in baskets. All this, while carrying our guns and our pouches.

All the pooralis would be soaked in sweat. This kind of work, under the burning sun, is extremely tough. Our leader [LTTE leader Pirapaaharan] would enthuse us by saying, 'What to do? It is our road. We are the ones who must build it and repair it.' He would join in the work too.

Even while doing such strenuous work, Ithayan would be clowning around. At times, others would give Ithayan a sand bath. When the sand sticks to his sweaty body he looks pretty pathetic.

The tractor trailer shook. It kept making a 'dong-dong' noise.

'God, why the hell are you driving so rough? Why can't

you drive slower?' Vasanthan pleaded. Salam laughed loudly in reply.

'From his laughter, it looks like he has decided to turn us inside out,' Ithayan said irritably. We could see the other tractor trailers following us at a distance. The one driven by David annai had only one headlight. It could be seen from afar.

I felt sad looking at the large paalai and veera trees. As they swayed in the wind, they appeared to be asking, 'Why are you leaving us?'

This was such a big forest. It had protected us like a mother all this time. When would we come back to it? Unable to hold back, I raised my hand and waved goodbye.

'What are you doing?' asked Vasanthan. He must have thought my brain had gone mushy with all the shaking in the tractor.

'Oh, nothing,' I said as I flicked the tears that were forming in my eyes. Drops fell on the red sand—the land soaked with our sweat.

Ithayan was dozing off, all the while holding up the light. I loosened my pouch and held up my T-58 [Chinese assault rifle]. Clouds were whizzing past over our heads.

The tractor trailer stopped at the camp at the end of the forest. Salam spoke to the poorali on guard at the sentry-post. He then took off at high speed.

'Salam, stop the tractor trailer. Vasanthan has fallen off. Idiot, what are you doing? What kind of driving is this?' Ithayan, yelling at the driver, got off and ran to the front of the vehicle.

Salam looked very worried. Before he could ask what had happened, Ithayan appeared in front, standing on the mudguard.

'Start the tractor trailer,' he shouted.

Salam realized in that second that Ithayan had fooled him. Defeated, he laughed as he put his foot on the accelerator. The tractor trailer took off like a jeep.

'These two idiots together are going to finish us off,' Vasanthan fumed. He was angry that his name was used in their tomfoolery.

Nayaru Bridge appeared at a distance like a large squatting animal.

'Machan, when the Indians were here we couldn't come anywhere near this place. If we had, our skulls would have been blown to smithereens,' remembered Vasanthan.

'However, we did give them a good beating here,' I reminded him.

'A lot of them were killed, weren't they?' Vasanthan raised the fact as a question.

'Yes, twenty-six army men died. We captured twenty-one weapons. Carlcustov [rocket-propelled gun], Bren [machine gun] were all captured,' I recalled.

Just before climbing on to a road, Salam drove the vehicle through a flooded hole. The big tyres splashed muddy water on Vasanthan and me. When Salam started to laugh, I got really angry.

'You mad man! See, the rifle has got wet,' I yelled at him.

'Sorry, I won't do it again,' apologized Salam.

Vasanthan spat the muddy water out of his mouth. A large black cloud hid the moon like a screen. The sky appeared empty.

'Look.' A shooting star shone bright and disappeared.

'What is it?' I tested Vasanthan.

'That is what people call a shooting star. One should not

look at one of those. If you do, then as remedy, you should look at any kind of tree that oozes milky sap.' Saying this, Vasanthan searched for such a tree to rest his eyes on.

But there were no trees as far as the eye could see. Vasanthan, who had grown up in a village, was influenced by such superstitions.

'That is rubbish. It is called an asteroid,' explained Ithayan. Vasanthan was not prepared to accept this reasoning. I managed to change the subject. Somehow the conversation drifted to home.

Salam's speed reduced as the tractor trailer climbed the Nayaru Bridge. The box-like armed trailer we were sitting on was very heavy. It was hard to pull. The tractor was struggling under its weight. We could see David annai's tractor trailer turning the bend as ours climbed uphill.

Vasanthan had become my best friend. He confided in me about everything. It is a kind of liberty assumed by fellow pooralis. Vasanthan began talking about his family.

'Appa, Amma, Thaaththaa, two younger brothers and three older sisters—that is my family. As far as I can remember, Appa used to drink. Although he did not drink every day, once a week he would come home with a large pot of toddy. He would be really excited about pouring the toddy into the container made of palmyra leaf and drinking out of it.

'He would make promises never to drink again, but soon after he would go to the toddy vendor. I cannot forget those days,' Vasanthan sighed. 'I had all these thoughts bottled up in my mind and I felt like letting them out today.'

I was surprised to see tears in Vasanthan's eyes. 'Why are you crying after telling us about such a close-knit family?' I asked, truly confused.

'No, but the troubles started after this. Thaaththaa got cancer. Appa was arrested by the army which accused him of hiding weapons by burying them in his tobacco plot. After six or seven days we identified his body by the earring he was wearing. The army had killed him using burning tyres.' Vasanthan looked away into the distance. 'I joined the movement after that. Amma is paralysed below the waist after the Indian Army shot her. My accas work at the vegetable plot to survive.'

A tractor wheel started to jump as it rotated.

'Boy, stop the tractor. Looks as if the tyre has a problem,' I said. The tractor stopped with a jerk. The nuts holding the tyres were broken. Only five of the eight nuts were in place.

'Let's go slow.' Salam changed gear.

The tractor started to crawl.

'A lot of Tamils lived in these parts. Everything was destroyed by bombs. How many boats and fishing nets they would have burned. Most of the people have now been displaced. Only a few are still here. They support us a great deal,' Vasanthan said.

At a distance, derelict huts with palm-leaf roofs that were decaying could be seen. Some of the huts had been knocked down. The odd stem from the decayed palm fronds swayed in the wind. Under the moonlight it appeared like some animal moving.

'Look there,' pointed Vasanthan. 'That is the way to small waterholes where rainwater collects. People survive by fishing in them. What can people do, if they cannot go to sea to fish?'

Along the edge of the waterhole huge lighted torches glowed in the dark. All at once a man threw a net. Another man was pulling the net he had cast earlier. As we sped past, people along the edge of the lake began to disappear. Their tormented faces stuck in my mind. Entire families were forced to come to this waterhole to catch whatever they could. The extent of poverty these people had been struck by dawned on me.

'Salam, switch off the lights!' Vasanthan, who was watching the sky, suddenly shouted.

When Vasanthan shouted a second time, Salam switched off the lights.

'What is the matter, machan? Is it a helicopter? Look carefully,' said Salam.

I used the torch to send the signal, and all five tractors behind us were darkened.

A helicopter cut across the moon in the sky. The pilot must have noticed the lights going off. He suddenly turned back and started to circle. Taking our weapons and other things, we crossed the road and ran. David annai ordered us to take our positions. I turned on the walkie-talkie, and went behind a tree with the poorali carrying the GPMG [general-purpose machine gun].

After a second circle, the helicopter began to dip. The pilot started operating his 50-mm-calibre machine gun and bullets roared past. Some hit the ground and exploded. David annai started to give orders.

'If he comes down give him one hundred with the big one,' he ordered.

Something suddenly whirred and then bhumm. . . .

'Machan, Para has made a hit; all lie flat. If he sees us, that will be the end. If you can, then move forward,' said David annai.

Salam, who was standing behind a sand mound, ran for

the tractor trailer. The helicopter started to pump it with five-inch artillery shells. Smoke rose from where the explosions came. The earth shook. Salam started the tractor trailer and pressed the accelerator. The helicopter descended upon the tractor trailer on the road. The pilot seemed to be thinking that it would be easy to fire at it from behind.

I shouted orders and the GPMG began to spit fire. The enemy did not expect this. The helicopter immediately rose up, all the while firing 50-mm-calibre shells.

'They got caught badly,' laughed Nesan.

The GPMG barrel was red-hot. He started to pick up the links used to hold the rifle bullets that had fallen off.

I remembered the words of our training master, Selvarasa, 'We are not a State military. We are pooralis. We do not have a lot of resources. We must be very frugal. Every bullet we use must kill an occupying enemy-soldier. We must avoid the wasteful use of arms.'

The tractor continued its journey. We were all scanning the skies in readiness. The helicopter could return or else they might try to obstruct us in some other way. A van came swiftly and stopped beside us. Salam pulled the tractor to one side to accommodate the van. Ramesh appa, our political head for the district, was seated in the passenger seat in front.

'What damage was caused by the helicopter strafing?' I queried.

'A five-inch shell killed one and injured two fishing at the waterhole.' With this, he sped off.

For a moment I thought of our district political heads and the senior politicians. I also remembered the family that was fishing at the waterhole. A teardrop fell on the rifle magazine. I shook off my (sad) mood and observed the road.

Sprawling across the fertile area of Alampil were huge coconut estates. These estates would give us enough income.

It was scary to see the tops of the coconut palms. They were spread out like umbrellas and seemed to be struggling to carry the large bunch of coconuts. Here and there, canopies of other large trees looked as if they were hills hanging in the sky. Water rushed in the canals. As the rushing water hit little rocks and leaped over them, the droplets seemed to turn into white pearls in the moonlight. The play of the rushing water acted as a tranquillizer. Water plants flourishing along the canals swayed in the breeze, filling the senses.

At the Alampil junction the tractor trailer turned into Kumulamunai road.

'Machan, drive carefully. The road is not very good; the vehicle can topple over,' said Vasanthan, as he turned back and looked at the sky.

The moon had come out of the clouds, and it lit up the whole firmament.

Along both sides of the Kumulamunai road, the paddy fields were overflowing with young green paddy shoots. Water-filled canals snaked through the fields. An alkaaddi flying above overtook us, screaming eerily.

Vasanthan reminisced, 'Does an alkaaddi never stop? My thaaththaa used to tell me that a screaming alkaaddi will not live for much longer. It screams for its mate, and falls somewhere and dies. I never asked Thaaththaa how all these alkaaddi birds are still flying. I wish I had, and put him on the spot.'

Six or seven palmyra trees stood forlornly at a distance.

It was 11.52 p.m.

It would take at least two days to reach our destination. Vasanthan stroked the T-81 [Chinese assault rifle], deep in thought.

We were on the bend on the straight Kumulamunai road. A naaval tree, with its fat roots, leaned over the road. Salam put both hands on the steering wheel and expertly turned it. He turned cautiously. Those hands were practised at this. His body turned with his hands.

Surely the turn was not so sharp that Salam had to be working that hard. Why was he turning so much? His body was showing signs of desperation. He yelled, fear-stricken, sweat running down his face.

'Jump, all of you! Jump off from behind! The steering rod is broken.'

I was at the back. I made a big leap. As I jumped off, I turned back to look. Vasanthan was dozing off; no, no, he was in a deep trance.

'Vasanthan, jump, man! The tractor trailer is going to hit something,' I yelled with all my strength.

My voice echoed off the trees in all directions. The trees shook once. The moon cried once. Birds on treetops flew off, shouting. Cows in the sheds mooed. Alkaaddi birds chased one another. A peacock screamed. The villagers woke up. A drop of blood splattered on me. As the tractor went over the roots of the naaval tree, the heavy trailer behind toppled on to the roadside. I ran towards it, yelling, 'Vasantha! Vasantha!' Salam and Ithayan were struggling to rescue our mate, our soulmate. Vasanthan was struggling for breath. It was a frightening sight.

We struggled to pull him out. I then turned towards the villagers' huts and shouted, half-crying: 'Won't someone come and help rescue my Vasanthan. . . .'

My scream tore through the wind and the gates, and woke up an amma, appa, acca and anna. 'Please come, please come,' I kept yelling.

In that beautiful thatched-roof hut, Vasanthan was lying on the only mattress. He was half-conscious. His right arm dangled below the shoulder; and his left hand, crushed, hung below the elbow. He breathed heavily. The two pillows under each arm—all the pillows in the hut—were soaked in blood. The amma took the teacup from the acca's hand and raised it to Vasanthan's lips. The old appa went to the cow to get some milk for Vasanthan.

David annai changed the antenna on his walkie-talkie and called for another vehicle.

In the meantime, a medical student in the village administered first aid to Vasanthan and gave him a Valium injection. This calmed him. My friend, who was always beside me and who always slept beside me, was now lying on the battleground. He started to talk to the acca who was sitting quietly. I wondered why he had started to talk all of a sudden.

'Acca, acca,' his voice dragged out.

'Yes, what is it, thambi?'

'You look very much like my acca, Viththi. What will my acca be doing now? She will be sleeping next to my little brother. They will be struggling with the daily work in the vegetable fields. All the trouble is due to the army, the Sinhalese. . . . Although my appa drinks, he is a good man. Aiyo. . . .' he moaned in pain.

The dog in the front yard slowly began to howl. Its howl pierced the soul. The tiny coconut-oil lamp struggled to stay alive. An insect fell on the flame, briefly making it brighter. It fell into the oil and died.

The sound of a vehicle floated past. The vehicle picked up Vasanthan. I was supporting Vasanthan; he was weak due to the heavy loss of blood. I stroked his rough cheeks and tried to say goodbye.

He cried, 'Leo, please, do not leave me.'

My heart followed the vehicle speeding away till it disappeared.

2

The People at Kumulamunai

10 November 1990

We took off to Kumulamunai in the vehicle that had just arrived.

It was 5.35 a.m.

Such big forests. The seasonal rainwater was flowing in the big channels forged by nature.

'Rainwater flows like this in these areas. Sometimes it flows over the roads. These floods can even topple big trees.' The driver appeared to have guessed that I am not from this area.

He stopped with a sudden brake near a bridge. 'Look, there is a crocodile lying on the log,' he pointed out.

'Where?' I couldn't see properly.

'On top of that big tree's branch,' he pointed.

A big crocodile was lying along the branch, camouflaged.

'It will stay like this. When prey, a goat or a cow, comes near, that is it. One day, when I was small, our cows and calves were out grazing. They went to drink water in the sun, at midday. A crocodile took away one of the calves. When all the other cows came back to their shed, these two, cow and calf, were missing.

'Appa sent Anna and me to look for them. We looked everywhere, but couldn't find them. When we went near the waterhole, we heard the cow's mournful cry. We went there and found the cow.

'Anna put the rope round its neck and pulled it. It refused to move. We went and told Appa. He came with two more people and dragged it home.'

'What happened then?' I asked.

'What else. The cow refused to eat and after some time it died.'

Vasanthan's mother came to my mind. Like the calf's mother, waiting for her offspring without eating—will Vasanthan's mother also . . . no, no. I consoled myself. I suddenly realized that we had come a long way from that bridge.

The vehicle passed several villages and then came to Mulliyavalai village. The morning dew was still hanging in the air. Visibility was poor. The vehicle was forced to move slowly. Along the road, the lanterns in the tea shops glowed. Their yellow light came intermittently through the mist. We stopped at a tea shop and had a hot cup of tea.

The shopkeeper's expression reflected his dislike of customers with bloodstained shirts. I remembered the amma who had given tea to the wounded Vasanthan. We got back into the vehicle.

The bund of the Murippu Tank came into view at a distance. On this side, wherever one looked, huge fields of paddy stretched like green silk.

The herons in the paddy fields took flight as the farmers' plough approached them. Something, suddenly, gave me a fright—a sad howling noise. It was the alkaaddi; it crossed the road and flew away. We got off the vehicle, but the alkaaddi's howl was still ringing in my head.

'Machan, I need a nap. Wake me up at noon,' I told my friends and spread the sack under a paalai tree, used my bag of books for a pillow, and fell asleep.

I woke up in a fright at 12.30 p.m. To my surprise, several schoolchildren had surrounded us. Ithayan and Salam were entertaining them. Typically, the children kept on questioning us non-stop. One little girl, nudging her brother, asked:

'Anna, how do you shoot this? Our appa's gun is long like a log, not like this one.'

'That is a different type, girl. Appa's is a shotgun. You can shoot only once with it. This can shoot all these bullets in one go.'

All the children looked at the boy who had answered.

'Can we look at the bullets?'

'Look at it and give it back.' Ithayan removed the magazine, took a bullet and held it out to the children. The children looked at it eagerly.

'I want one like this.'

'Not now. You can have one when you are a grown-up.'

'How many armies did you shoot?'

'Why do you shoot the army? Poor army.'

'Then why did the army shoot my uncle and grandpa?'

'Who told you that the army shot them?'

'The army men shot them when I was little and lying in my Amma's lap. The man came inside the house and shot them. Amma's hands also got wounded. My uncle used to take me to the shop and buy me sweets. Once when I was sick, he went and brought the doctor at midnight. That is what Amma told me.'

'Yes, I cried a lot. Amma used to tell me not to cry. Amma said when I grow up I must shoot the army. Will the army take me too before I grow up?'

Tears welled up in my eyes. Ithayan embraced the child.

'Why are we here? We will certainly kill them.' Ithayan's words were heated; the frightened child pulled back. Ithayan pulled the child and embraced her again. Salam yawned.

'Anna, when did you eat?'

I wondered if the traditional practice of asking 'What did you eat?' had changed now to 'When did you eat?'

'Haven't eaten since last night,' Salam said, using sign language. Greedy man!

The children looked at our weapons for a long time, and then said goodbye and left. We kept waving to them until they disappeared, like butterflies.

An amma carrying a pot of water on her hip and accompanied by a little girl with a bag was walking in our direction. The sun was hot, and the two were walking barefoot.

'What are we going to do for food, machan?'

'Try calling on the walkie-talkie. I doubt there will be food. Probably we will have to starve today. I know it is hard for you after eating three good meals a day in the forest,' Ithayan took a dig at Salam.

Salam, already hungry, threw a stick at Ithayan.

'That amma is coming towards us.'

Exhausted, the amma put the pot down and smiled fondly at us.

'Sons, all of you look tired. You all look as if you did not sleep last night. Wash your hands with the water from the pot and eat. It is not good for your health to go without sleep and food.' The amma smiled as if she knew everything. The little girl put the bag down and went to look at our weapons.

'Careful, little one; it will explode.'

'No, it won't,' the little one laughed.

'Have you eaten?'

'Not yet. You eat first; I will eat later.'

'No. Let us all eat together.'

Ithayan picked up the little one and put her on his lap. She had just got back from school and had only had a drink of water. Amma mixed the food into small balls and placed it in our hands. We finished the food. Yoghurt and ghee, the smell was heavenly.

'Excellent. Wonderful.' This was Salam.

Once his stomach was full, Salam became curious.

'What are Amma's children doing?'

'The eldest is with you all. This is the second one. That is all,' she said.

Five or six more ammas came to us with food. We struggled to eat and begged them to stop feeding us.

Is this the food of love? I don't know. By 6.30 p.m. half of Kumulamunai village was there to wave us goodbye.

Unwilling to sit in the trailer, I went and sat in front on the mudguard. The vehicle shook and started to move—without Vasanthan. I looked back. I wondered if Vasanthan had been taken to Jaffna. I was sure Vasanthan would be fighting in the upcoming battle on the frontline. Could he have died? No, no, I didn't think so.

All three of us were quiet as the wheels swallowed the distance. The sun started to disappear in the west. The sky looked as if it was painted red. But the painter was careless; his brush had touched the white clouds, giving the clouds a red tinge. Paint drops must have fallen into the water puddles amidst the fields because they too were slightly reddened.

A white heron was flying in the reddened wind. Herds of cows were returning home. A calf kept tugging at her mother's udders, annoying her. I couldn't bear to look. Something hurt inside.

'Machan, stop next to that man with the gun.'

The vehicle slowed and stopped. They looked like a father and son. The iya looked seventy. His son must have been forty-five. They were standing outside their home, chatting with their family.

'What can we do for you, boy?' the iya asked.

'Oh, nothing. Our water-can tipped over. We stopped to check it,' I replied.

'Bloody liar,' Ithayan mumbled.

I fiddled with the tank and listened to what the family was saying.

'When will you come back?' the amma asked. She must be the wife of the iya.

'Thankam, we have to leave now in a hurry. We can't be sure when we will be back. Have you got everything you need at home?'

'Yes, everything is here. Our grandson has been running a fever for two days. I am worried about him.'

'If there is an emergency, call the man next door; he will help. I will tell him about it before I leave.'

The daughter-in-law came out of the house.

'What did you cook?' the son asked his wife.

'Puttu and fish curry. I cooked your favourite food.'

He looked at his wife fondly.

'Our son's fever is not going down. If you come back quickly, we can take him to the doctor at Mulliyavalai.'

'Amma, the little one has vomited,' said the little boy's older sister.

'Appa, wait a minute.' The old man's son ran inside and picked up his little son, his wife standing next to him. He kissed the child and handed him to his wife.

'I will be back soon. But do not wait for me. Go quickly and get the medicine.'

'Appa, how many army men will you shoot this time?' the child asked his father.

'We don't keep count, boy. I will shoot every army man and thug that comes here as long as I have life in my body.'

'If there is no life in your body?' the child queried.

'Why do you think you are here? If I die, you must shoot them. If you don't, they will take or destroy everything of ours. You will then be living at the mercy of someone else.'

'Then why didn't you teach me to shoot?'

'If you shoot, the gun will pull you with it. When you are bigger you can learn.' He turned to his wife. 'We will be going. Take the boy and get the medicine.'

Father and son walked closer to us. We offered to give them a ride.

'Keep talking to the iya. I will go and get some water,' I said and walked towards the house.

'Amma, water,' I said, and the older girl took our can inside.

She immediately came running back. 'Amma, the mother cow is not in the shed. All the others are there.'

Mother put a hand over the girl's mouth and silenced her.

'Don't shout when Appa is just leaving; we will go and look.'

A white cow came along the road with its calf and passed me.

'Oh, they are here.' The little boy ran to them, put his hands around the cow's neck and began kissing her. The cow licked the boy back. The calf brushed its body against the boy.

I took the can of water, thinking about the boy's determination to protect his motherland for this love. I wondered about the people in this sacred land that connects the north and the east of the Tamil homeland.

I could hear the old man talking.

'We have been fighting the Sinhalese since the 1950s. They came to Chemmalai and we beat them back[1]. We rescued our people who were tied up. We burned down the settlers' huts. When the police came we hid in the jungles. They took four of our people and charged them in the courts, but they were released.'

He paused, 'Later, it was the army that tormented our people and pursued them. Stop here; we will get off.'

Both the father and son started to walk through the paddy fields. I looked at Ithayan and we smiled. Before we joined our armed revolution, these older folk had been fighting the Sinhalese who tried to split the Tamil homeland into two. Had our politicians of that time supported these brave men, it would have made a big difference; had our politicians guided them along a revolutionary path, our land would have been free.

With my thoughts and the vehicle speeding away, we carried on with our journey.

[1]Sinhalese fishermen had been coming to Tamil fishing areas for centuries for seasonal fishing. Until the 1950s the relationship between the two groups had remained amicable because there were plenty of resources and the settlers were temporary. The planned incursions with assistance from the Lankan military started around the 1950s. The old man in this conversation is referring to one particular incident in Chemmalai between the two groups.

3

Army in My Village

10 November 1990

The moonlight had started to spread. Stars twinkled. We continued our journey through it all. The roads were in very poor condition. Since ours was the vehicle that needed the most repairs, we had sent forward all the other vehicles before us, and were proceeding very slowly.

My thoughts were taken up by Vasanthan. Salam drove quietly, avoiding potholes and water puddles. We passed Murippu and went over big bridges. We were now driving through the Poothan rice fields towards Thaneeroottu.

'Machan, this is the Katpahapillaiyaar temple. I used to come here a lot in my younger days. An old man used to conduct bhajan sessions here every Friday,' I said.

We went past the cooperative shop and the rice mill, and went over a big water canal. I pointed to a place.

'This is where we were living. It is exciting to see the place after so many years. That neem tree hosts scores of monkeys. I used to be very timid when I was young. Appa and his friends used to sit on the front porch and chat.'

We passed the Mulliyavalai Viththiyaananthaa College

and went on. I thought of the people of Manalaaru near the waterholes. We must trounce the enemy on Maaveerar Day. We must create a situation where they cannot stay in our land any more.

Ithayan and I complained that we were sleepy.

'Do you know what will happen if I fall asleep?' Salam said with a smile. He pointed to the big canal next to the road which was full of water.

'Good grief, we can't let this fellow fall asleep,' Ithayan said. 'What is this, machan? They have put a banner here,' he continued.

'This is the Oddusuddaan police station; the army was here earlier,' I replied.

'When were they beaten?'

'In 1990.'

'Wasn't this place overrun by our boys earlier as well?'

'Yes, in 1985. That, too, was a good beating. We captured a lot of rifles. Saba annai and Lawrence annai led that attack.'

Signs of army occupation were still evident. Walls were damaged, and in some places they had been completely destroyed. A broken board said 'Military Remand Camp'.

'Slow down, man. Let us have a look,' I said. I began explaining the camp layout to my friends.

'I know this camp a little. In 1986, my brother was arrested and kept here. I was small then. I would come here with Amma and cry. This is the main entrance. They would open this gate only for their big vehicles. See that big tree there? That is the first sentry-post. Those days they used trees and bricks rather than sandbags to build sentry-posts. Sometimes they kept watch from trees.

'The next sentry on the other side of the road would be posted at the Muthaiyankaddu junction. In between, the road would be deliberately dug up to create potholes. At some places they would put drums to block the road. That big water tank turned upside down, sitting on the ground, was one of tallest things around here. They put sandbags on it and an observation-sentry would be there. You could see all around from there. If they saw anyone, they would come at you like hunting dogs.

'Look at all these buildings. One wouldn't know which building the enemy would be hiding in. There would be barbed-wire fences all around. They would be surrounded again with rolls of barbed wire. After that there would be trenches.'

Then, reminded of an incident of torture that I witnessed, I described it to the others.

'It was the fourth day after the army took away my brother. It was 6 a.m. We came here on the early morning bus. It was cold. We were making inquires to the sentry about him when we saw a boy. There was this bed made of barbed wire, fixed six inches from the ground on poles. This boy was made to lie on it, face down and was tied to it. He lay very still. A little later, seven or eight people came. One of them in the middle was big. He put his boots on the back of the boy. The boy screamed. Man, even the elephant couldn't scream so loud.

'The big man stood on the boy's body and grabbed his hair and pulled it. The big man acted like he was riding a horse. I can't describe the way the boy screamed. The man then let go of the boy's hair and got hold of his forehead and pulled the boy backwards. The boy's cry, 'Amma', was from one half dead. His neck hung like that of a rooster with a broken neck. He didn't move after that.

'Blood started to drip underneath the barbed wire. Amma quickly dragged me away, but I looked back. Two people removed him from the barbed wire and took him away. Blood was dripping from his body. His broken neck was hanging.

'That is when I saw another fifteen people within an area fenced off with barbed wire. They were all being beaten with logs. Amma dragged me and ran out. The sentry whistled and laughed as we ran out. How can I forget?'

I went near a barbed-wire fence to look. I am not sure if it was blood, but there were dried red patches on the barbed wire. I kicked the wire angrily, and took Ithayan and walked away.

A board inscribed with the letters 'LTTE' smiled at us in the moonlight. We paid our respects at the maaveerar memorial at the junction.

We turned into a narrow lane. 'Stop in the thick jungle; it will be daylight soon,' I said.

Salam started to look for an entry into the thick jungle. 'Stop here.'

Salam reversed and stopped at a perfect spot not visible from the road. We were all cold in the clothes that had got wet in the rain. We had not eaten since 6 p.m. yesterday. Not even a hot cup of tea. It was now 3.20 a.m. All three of us, Salam, Ithayan and me, were affected by this.

A strange sound was issuing from Ithayan.

'What the hell is the matter?' I asked.

We shone the torchlight on him. A red-ants' nest had fallen and the ants had got disturbed. They were all over Ithayan's body, biting him, and dying in the process.

'Come outside and take off your shorts.' All three of us were brushing the ants off his body. Ithayan looked pathetic.

All his friends back in his village would be asleep now. What does that say about Ithayan? Had life betrayed him? No. History had showed him the way to live. He must live here so future generations can breathe freely. The jungle was his protection. This was his joy.

'What are you thinking, machan? Let us sleep outside.'

Both of us lay down. Ithayan was in misery. He lay moaning for a long time because of the pain from the ant bites. My turn at sentry duty came up. I picked up my rifle, dropped my nap, and started patrolling. The cold pierced through my polythene coat.

The moonlight started to fade. Clouds hurried away. The sky slept. Faint noises indicated some activity now and then. A peacock called. I heard something familiar far away. My heart longed for something. Yes, it was the alkaaddi. It must be searching for its mate.

I was suddenly taken aback by noises nearby. The noise was getting nearer. A foul odour filled the air.

'Salam, machan, something is coming. Looks like an elephant.'

About seventy-five metres away, a black hill stood blocking the lane. Two eyes sparkled in the dark. I could hear the elephant's tail swishing away the flies. The elephant turned in our direction and lifted its trunk.

'Mate, we can't run away now; it is too close. Wake up Ithayan, then run to the tractor, start it and focus the light on its eyes.'

I loaded the T-81 and cocked it, ready to shoot a single bullet. In the light of the tractor, the eyes sparkled even more. The elephant started moving towards the light.

'It is dangerous now. You run with Ithayan. I will take care of this,' I told Salam.

The elephant drew nearer and nearer. Killing wild animals will damage our natural resources. Our trainer in the forest had told us several times to be cautious about killing wildlife. I ran fast behind Salam. But we weren't going to make it.

Bang.

A bullet went over the elephant's head. It paused and then trumpeted, and started chasing us even faster.

I had to now. Had to shoot.

Ithayan had fallen over a log, and he let out a scream. Salam helped him up. The elephant was just forty-five metres away. I aimed for its forehead. It fell down like a black hill. I sighed, feeling sad. Salam started his sentry duty. As morning came and the birds began singing, I fell asleep.

11 November 1990

I was woken up at 9.30 a.m. We contacted the nearby camp by walkie-talkie, and food arrived. The bread was slightly moist and the curry tasted strange. Salam's face said it all.

'You know, annai, you are far away from our camp. Breakfast will arrive here only at 11 a.m. This is last night's dinner,' said Easan, the poorali who had brought the food.

I took a bite of the bread and poured water from the can into the cup. I could see motes floating in the water.

'Do you have water problems?' I asked.

'Yes, annai. The well is very deep, and, somehow, the

green water-fungus spreads in the well. This water is boiled, cooled and filtered; still, a few floaters get through.'

'Okay, that is all right. Are you in contact with David annai?'

'Yes, he made contact at 8.10 a.m. Finish your food, and let's go. People won't come here. There are sentries around. They won't let anyone in.'

We hid the 'big item' under bushes where there would be no movement of people. We climbed into the truck brought by the poorali and sped towards Maankulam.

Easan pointed to a tall stick-like thing and laughed, saying, 'This is the enemy tower.' As we got closer, we could see that it was held upright by several tight ropes stretched in all directions.

The truck turned slowly into a lane.

'Can we not go straight on to the main road?'

'If you go there, not even small pieces of you will be left. Beyond that curve, everything is the enemy's target. He will shoot even a dog that strays there.'

The lane was in bad shape. 'Can't we go along this?' I pointed at another way.

'We used to go that way. One day they fired at our jeep. Five people were injured. So now we have orders not to take vehicles. One can walk, though.'

The truck stopped in front of a camp. It was 2.30 p.m. We had lunch. Jeevan came and took us around the camp. The three of us were together and Ithayan's face lit up with happiness.

It was hard to say if the pain of the ant-bites had gone or he was just ignoring it. Dried blood covered the wound from his fall last night. His pants were ripped. We walked along the main road. The houses were all damaged by the shelling and bombing.

One hut was totally burned down. Clay pots and pans—charred and in pieces—were lying scattered. A sari—badly faded and in shreds—hung on the fence. It spoke of the haste in which their owners had run away.

A mango tree was standing, charred on one side. The other side of the tree was sprouting new shoots. It must have been an aerial bomb. On top of the ash heap in the front yard, green grassy shoots were coming out. How was that possible? I was surprised. After a shower, the birds must have dropped the seeds.

Next to the hut a bigger house, its roof shattered, looked bright as the daylight shone through the gaps on top. The crown of a coconut tree had got partially lopped off and hung from its trunk.

Enemy camps create many problems for us. Militarily, such camps restrict our movement. The enemy's strategy of harassment costs us lives and ammunition.

That is not all.

There are political effects too. The enemy is also able to boast that he controls the economic life of the civilians. The camps create economic problems for our people. Displacement also causes economic losses. Those displaced are forced to start all over again in new places. Their energies are wasted. So much cultivable land lies unused because of these camps. The displaced languish without land.

Because of multiple upheavals, people have been unable to develop their skills in agriculture. The camps also block transportation routes. This has an economic cost as longer routes are taken. How can a Tamil Eelam be established if there are such economic embargoes? We cannot permit these to continue.

There are cultural impacts too. Many camps are built around temples. The temple walls provide cover.

'This is Maankulam Mahaviththiyaalayam.'

Jeevan pointed to the school. The big school had not been damaged much. The grass on the playground had grown waist-high. Soon this would become a jungle.

Oh, my dearest little brothers and sisters, where are you all? We know that the enemy does not like your young feet stepping into schools. He doesn't want to see you carrying books. The enemy is bent on destroying the backbone of the Tamil community: their education.

I know you will be huddled somewhere in a little hut or a building to avoid the rain. But you will be drenched because the huts have only palm-leaf roofs which are thoroughly decayed. You will not be eating lunch. Your little stomachs will ache due to hunger.

Come here again in a few days. Wash your tiny feet in

these water tanks. I will come like a big wave looking for you. I will put your feet in this school. I will cushion your tiny feet from the earth. I will embrace you like a breeze while you are studying.

We cautiously studied the enemy set-up.

Bang . . . bang. Bullets went over our heads.

'Machan, lie down. He has seen us. He is firing from the tamarind tree over there. He will fire for a little while and then he will come down.

'Come, let us go; but keep low.' Jeevan ran in front and we followed.

BOOM! A shell fell on the spot where we had been lying down.

Our man at the security-post said, laughing, 'He is angry because we cut off his supplies. For one week we fired 50-mm-calibre shots, preventing the supply helicopter from landing. He is angry.'

We began identifying the targets through each of the enemy security-posts. Jeevan pointed to every enemy security-post and gave us an explanation.

'The road going past the temple security-post is the Mullaitheevu road that comes up here. That thing in the corner is a shop. Next to it is the Buddhist Vihara. Beyond that is his old camp.'

In front, a cement wall half-eaten by bullets carried the sign, 'Army Camp'.

A poorali standing next to us laughed, 'It is here my father and I were stopped and threatened as we were returning from Maankulam on our way home.'

Oh, the child you threatened once, the young shoot you stepped on, the Tamil you teased, is standing with a gun in front of you. His presence is taking you by surprise. How can you understand that it is the occupier who creates a poorali? You once dealt the blow. Now you are imprisoned. When a fox tries to eat the goat, the goat must turn into a tiger and leap. That is the edict of the times.

Jeevan carried on with his explanations.

'On the other side of the camp is a mango orchard. Inside are eight security-posts. Some of them are dummy posts. But we should fire at them as well so they don't know that we are aware they are dummy posts. Over that way, towards the Luxabana, you can see the mountain security-post. Since it is at a good height, he can cover all the open space. I think it could be with a 50 mm calibre or an L3 [double-barrelled machine gun].'

The camp certainly was strong. The enemy must have calculated that the large open space surrounding his camp meant that during movement across the land we would have to suffer heavy losses.

We had cut off the Thunukkai road just before the junction. It looked as if the enemy had done the same in front of his camp. It could be his supply route or it could even be fake. We had put screens at places where we had a direct view of the enemy. We were watching through the branches of the tamarind tree at the junction.

'Don't look there for too long: he will snipe at you,' warned Jeevan.

'What you see at this end is the church. That is the nuns' hostel. Those are houses. All those security-posts protect the camp on this side. That is what made it possible for helicopters to land. The enemy captured this only after the 1990 battle.'

'These security-posts appear to be rather close. Can't they be attacked with RPGs [rocket-propelled gun(s)] and separated?' I asked.

'It may look like they are close, but all are well-fortified security-posts. He has stacked huge quantities of sandbags. There are sandbags even behind the walls. The temple security-post is stronger than the others.'

These places of worship stood before us like horrendous enemies. Used for unjust purposes, they stood there, silent and grim. 'It is better to be destroyed than to assist the oppressor.' These words of an unknown philosopher came to my mind. We had to capture these two camps at any cost. After that there would be no question of helicopters landing. Earlier, this camp was only 100 × 200 metres. Now it had expanded to 1000 × 15,000 metres. Over and above this, the enemy had planted landmines in the open space.

The four of us walked towards the railway station security-post.

'Careful; he fires when we walk past the railway gates. Those sandbags have holes. Bend down and walk.'

As if the enemy had heard Jeevan, the machine gun started spitting.

'Ah . . .' There was no sound after that. We ran. Bullets whizzed over our heads.

'Gosh . . .' David annai laughed with a sigh as we joined him. Salam held his leg, laughing.

'Are you hurt, machan?'

'No, no, it just brushed past.'

Below the knee, some flesh was missing.

'Bring that field compressor.'

Jeevan bandaged Salam perfectly. I noticed only then that my rubber sandals were missing. One was lying on the railway track, broken. The other sandal was lying a bit farther away. I said goodbye to them.

'Be careful when you look; otherwise he will not let us sleep at night,' laughed the poorali at the security-post.

'That building on the main road on our side is the hospital. The building next to it is the hospital quarters. The next one is the bank. On that side of the road is the police station. Then comes the cooperative milk shop. Four or five buildings past the cooperative are warehouses for paddy. The enemy is in all of these buildings, but they are not well-fortified security-posts.

'He has many dummy posts. Off and on he will climb on trees and snipe. The one who shot at us a moment ago was from that post. The police station is on that side of the warehouse. From here, you cannot see it that well. Tomorrow we will go round and look from the Kanakaraayan Tank-end.'

'Do they occupy all these houses?'

'Yes, they are in all these houses.'

'Is that an army man? Oh, yes . . . he is hiding behind the bushes. Looks like he is urinating.'

Jeevan turned around. 'Machan, what type of rifle do you have?'

He took the G3 [assault rifle] that was handed to him. I asked whether I should provide support fire, and Jeevan nodded. Salam counted, 'One, two . . .' Bang. . . . Two explosions sounded together. We pulled back our rifles. He fell down.

'They will be coming to collect him and we can get them too.'

Two of them came running to pick up the fallen soldier. They suddenly stopped and said something to each other and then came forward fast.

'One is going to smash this place with an LMG [light machine gun] as the other picks up the body. Come, let us move to the other security-post.' I sped in front.

They had come close to the fourth post. They came closer. Bang. Before we could fire, his LMG began ripping the first post.

They picked up the body. Our G3 and T-81 spat fire. We lowered our guns and our heads, and ran towards the three fallen bodies. We collected some of their weapons and rejoiced at the collection.

Bullets started to test the sandbags in our security-posts. The noise got louder. We lowered ourselves into the trenches. Three shells fell close. One side of the security-post was all smoke. As the smoke lifted, the security-post stood there steady. Sand was pouring out from some of the sandbags.

All three bodies still lay there. We waited till dusk and then started to move.

'Let's look at the rest in the morning. We can now go along the road. He won't fire at night.'

A peacock called in the distance. Stars twinkled. We entered the Maankulam railway station. Tickets were strewn everywhere. The walls, soaked in the seasonal rain, had many bullet holes. The naked sky was visible through the damaged roof. Broken ceiling-beams hung in the air.

'Last week a shell fell on this building. If you look you can see the convent. He snipes from there in the daytime.'

Through the window, we saw the walls were pitted with bullet holes. Some of the window frames were broken. Each one of these bullets were indeed sent to destroy the pooralis who love this land, who dedicate themselves to protect this land. They were sent to destroy our pooralis. We are also sending the same copper bullets. But we send them to destroy the outsider occupying it.

'Man, I smell something in here.'

Salam opened the door. God! A dog killed by a shell was rotting. I was barely able to bear the smell, but I forced myself to take a peek. Once this brown dog with thick hair around its neck would have been the beloved pet of a family, and a dear friend to its children. It would have walked with the mother of the family as she went to the fields carrying food. It might have walked the children to and from school. Now it was lying dead with a bloated stomach. I pulled my head back from the door and slammed it shut.

4

The Enemy Camp

12 November 1990

'Wonder why there is so much smoke from their camp. Maybe they are cooking something good to eat before they die.' When Jeevan said this we all went over to see.

'Come, let's go forward and look. Remember to crawl flat on the ground. The sentry will be smoking his cigarette and looking elsewhere. Such is their sense of duty. Do not make noise. If he hears something, you will be riddled with bullets.'

We crawled behind the naayuruvi bush, becoming one with the ground.

Two bodies, one lying across the other, were burning. About ten feet away was a Sinhala soldier. He puffed at his cigarette with his AK-LMG slung over his shoulder. He was wearing long boots and his eyes were red. He walked away and then turned back. The camp looked ordinary.

Would he see us? For a minute, the hair on the backs of our necks pricked us. I was not sad to die. But there was so much to be done before I died. The soldier leaned on the sandbags. The bushes by the side of the railway line moved.

36

I straightened. He removed his AK-LMG and leaned it against the sandbags. 'Ah . . .' The next minute his rifle was going at full tilt until all the bullets in the link were finished.

Shameful. This can't be the military; these are undisciplined animals, rowdies. We turned and began crawling away. The sentry at the road fired a few times to show that he was there. We started to walk along the road. The smell of burning corpses lingered. If this undisciplined army got out of the camp, it would empty barrels of bullets into civilians. The thorns pricking our feet were painful; so were our hearts.

It was 9 a.m. We had to leave now in order to reach our location before lunchtime.

'If their camp was not there we would get there in five minutes.'

With Steiner binoculars hanging on his shoulder, Jeevan walked in front.

'Where are the rest of your people?' Jeevan asked one of his subordinates.

'They have gone to the other side.'

He understood the language. How many items? Again he understood the hand signs. We had to start our other preparations quickly. Jeevan squinted to observe the camp far away.

'If we finish early and complete the camouflage then there will be no problem. Let's go this way, rather than get fired at like yesterday.'

The military security-posts looked like tiny pyramids at a distance. The aerial stood tall and shone in the sun's rays. I gritted my teeth and told myself it would not be standing there for long.

We left the main road and walked over a bridge and came to an abandoned house. We crossed the fence and began walking along a footpath through the rice fields. Jam-fruit bushes reached up to our waist and their cool green leaves helped to hide us. Would the enemy fire a 50-mm calibre or would he shell? We crossed the rice fields and climbed on to Thunukkai road.

'Look here; can you see the burned spot?'

'Yes, yes, two or three months ago, army men were dropped off by helicopter and there was heavy fighting. This is where the bodies of the army men were burned after they were killed.'

'How did he drop the men without being seen?'

'We knew that if we blocked the helicopter from landing in this camp then he would drop the men somewhere behind it. One day, early in the morning, four helicopters dropped men exactly where we expected them to, in front of the Katkulam Lake. There were only a few of our pooralis there at that time. He started firing all around the forest, from the helicopter. There were about one hundred and fifty pooralis. Immediately, he began breaking the defence. We sent out the standby group as well. Most of the army men made it to their camp. Eight bodies of the army men were burned here. It was only after this that he bombed all these areas and captured them.'

'Did he capture what we had?'

'Yes, yes. Since we did not have a strong camp nor manpower, he took the police station, eye hospital, community hall, church, temple, bank, post office, milk board, paddy warehouses and all.'

Even Che Guevara advised withdrawal when one's strength was diminished. If we hadn't withdrawn we would have sustained heavy losses. We walked round the bend on Thunukkai road and climbed in a line on to the Katkulam

Lake bank. We were in the direct line of vision of the army's antenna. The lake was fairly broad. There were no lilies in the lake. In places in the lake, tall trees grew in clumps. Their leaves had dropped off and they were bare. The dried leaves had collected along the edge of the lake. Water crows sat on the trees and looked around. The sluice gate of the lake looked rusted.

Something jumped into the water from a log.

'Look, a crocodile has jumped in.' He pointed to the back of the crocodile.

There are no lakes without crocodiles, we all agreed and walked on. Lots of tiny fish played in the water overflowing from the tank. A white heron spread its wings and landed softly near the overflowing water. Fish gathered under the shadow of its wing to avoid the sun.

'Goodness, what a lot of paddy fields are lying fallow!'

'People won't come to cultivate. They are frightened.'

'Would we have walked two kilometres?'

Jeevan laughed. 'Probably one kilometre.'

The next lake-bank was almost vertical to the path. In front lay the vast Samiyaar Lake. Trees, tilting with large canopies, provided good shade. The water was covered with tiny lilies. We waited there for a while. Here, too, the trees standing in water were rotting. These very trees would have longed for water in the dry summer months. Now they were about to be engulfed by the water. Soon it would be joyfully leaping up to swallow them. Looking at the trees, I felt sorry for them.

The soft grass was a welcome change for our feet, sore after walking over stones. Why are you crying, feet? There is only a little bit more to go. It was getting frustrating. We pushed aside the bushes and walked. We could see ruined, burned huts in the distance. We were not happy to see them like that, but we were happy to have arrived. We started walking along a footpath. There used to be a settlement next to the forest behind the police station. The people who had lived here must have been landowning farmers. The houses were built either with mud or bricks. All the houses in the settlement had been destroyed by shelling. We passed the wells and walked on a path in front of one of the houses. The hibiscus was in full bloom on either side of the footpath. The trunk of a jackfruit tree lay broken. The walls on one side of the house were completely gone. It was in a bad state. There must have been children in the house. There were school books scattered everywhere. A Pillaiyar picture, a picture of god Ganesha, with its frame broken, lay on the ground.

We passed the hut and arrived at our post in front. On one side was a trailer piled with wooden planks. Pooralis were bringing them down from the trailer. I will never forget these moments. It was 10.45 a.m. Young pooralis, without even having breakfast, were toiling to carry those heavy planks. I noticed that they were tired and hungry. In spite of this there was determination on their faces. Every now and then they would put the planks on the ground and look at each other.

'This is as heavy as a dead body! It feels like our arms will break,' said one of them, and sat on a thick exposed root and pressed his bruised hands.

I later learnt that his name was Kannan.

'Prasanth, I am feeling giddy. Bring me some water,' said another poorali.

He drank some water which brought a smile to his face.

'We must finish this work today. Come on, quick. We must unload everything and send the tractor away. If helicopters come they will fire at it.'

The young poorali who had drunk the water walked past me, carrying a wooden plank together with Kannan. The hunger which I felt earlier was now gone. We crept along quietly, our heads covered with Hessian sacks, and observed the enemy camp.

'This security-post of ours has not really been noticed yet. Be careful when you look out. If he sees you, it will be hard to continue to work here,' the young poorali said as he gave us water.

'Not a problem, boy,' said Jeevan.

'What you see in front is the police station. There are four or five houses in front. There are several dummy posts too. That one, made of wooden planks, he has hidden with palm leaves. There is a good post at the water tower. There are more people in this corner building.'

'What is that on the other side of the road?'

'That is the last post. It is on the roadside. You know, annai, at night in this building they will be singing baila songs. They are not at all alert,' the young poorali said.

He placed the wooden planks down and brushed the dirt off himself.

'Okay. This side is done. Now to complete the rest of the work. Let's go to that side, to the roadside post,' he said.

Past the smaller houses there stood a bigger house, above the railway line along the road. I noticed only then that there were women-pooralis there.

'Are there girls at this post?'

'Oh, they came only a week ago.'

'You will be shot if you go that way,' a woman-poorali warned us, pointing towards the army camp.

We looked over the fence. The army security-post on the hill looked strong. We ran to avoid detection as we reached our roadside security-post. This was a very important post. If the enemy was going to advance he would use this path. The bombers would also target this post. The post stood firm across the road, under the command of women-pooralis who were ready to meet any land attack. They looked confident with their RPG 30-calibre rifles.

We looked at the other security-posts and at 1.45 p.m. we turned back towards our main camp.

'This evening we will go and look at the posts under Seeramaan and Sathiyaraj. They are very close by,' said Jeevan.

At lunchtime, after having what was meant for breakfast, we started off for the security-posts by the temple. We walked through a narrow lane. On both sides paddy fields and vegetable fields spread far. The uncultivated paddy fields were overgrown with weeds. In the vegetable plots there was an occasional pumpkin creeper and some rotting plantain trees, but everything else was overrun by weeds. There were huge spreads of mango orchards. All kinds of mangoes were in fruit. We stepped into a mango orchard and picked some; eating them we walked on. The sun was hot.

'We need to set up two posts on this side. Let us look for a good location,' I said.

We left the narrow lane and walked through the house yards. I managed to cope because I had got hold of another pair of rubber sandals. We crossed a palmyra estate and could see our post on the other side. With the poorali at the security-post, we started to view each of our posts.

'This is the post farthest from the army. It has a wide open space in front so we have pulled it back,' said Jeevan.

'Only from this post one can see the road-facing side of the temple, and the buildings on the Mullaitheevu road,' Jeevan was looking out as he said this.

'Yes. Is it a Pillaiyaar temple? Can see that clearly too. Looks like the posts are set up more tightly on this side. And they continue in a long line. The supply trenches must be here too,' I speculated.

'Yes, this temple post is precious to the enemy. Therefore all their set-ups will be here. From his post to this place is open space. He would have laid mines all over it. The team attacking from this side will meet with stiff resistance. Since there is this open space, his surveillance will be stronger on this side. One will have to face plenty of bullets, not to mention the landmines. Over and above all this, aerial attacks also will most likely be entirely on this side. There is a high chance of heavy losses,' said Jeevan.

Yet, if we were to capture the camp, we had to destroy the two main enemy camps at the temple and the inn adjoining it. Only then could we stop the supply to him by air, and besiege him. We had to capture this place whatever the cost to poorali lives. This, I thought, would be the deciding factor. I decided that the cannon would play an important role. The Luxabana electricity towers passed by us, went through the enemy area and then disappeared—tiny specks in the distance.

'The enemy is stationed along a distance of seven or eight towers,' Jeevan said.

We crossed, bending very low, to the security-post across the road. He could snipe. The piece of hessian sack on my head, how many holes it had. It now looked like a sieve. The temple post was clearly visible. Everyone stretched to look. After everyone else, I climbed up to look.

Woing. . . . A bullet whizzed past, twenty centimetres above my head. Like a tortoise retracting its head into its shell, I pulled my head in and climbed down. Without realizing it, I felt for the top of my head.

'He could have given you a big bindi, a vermilion mark, through your forehead. You just escaped,' said Jeevan, laughing.

We told the voice on the walkie-talkie that we were fine. We ran on the straight road, all the while bending low. About sixty men were filling sandbags and digging bunkers.

'Who are these people?'

'They come to help from different villages. Fifty of them come each day. These men are from the village of Muththaiyankaddu.'

The men were busy working. I could hear the commands and questions.

'Maarkandu, hold the sack.'

'Put another bag; I can carry it.'

'Is this broad enough or should it be widened?'

'Bring the spade here.'

Enthusiastic voices continued to be heard. They did not pay attention to the noise of firing. An old man who had just finished digging the trench, shook the dirt off his sarong and came and sat next to me on the side of the road.

'Iya, what are you doing in Muththaiyankaddu?' I asked him.

'Thambi, I am a retired school teacher. I was the headmaster of Mullivaikal School. After I retired, I came to Muththaiyankaddu for its peace and quiet. It is a good place. The weather is good. The hospital is nearby. I bought the house five years ago. So I am okay.'

I gave him the water-can and he took two gulps of water and returned the can with thanks. I was wondering how to start the conversation.

'Iya, how many children do you have?'

'I had two children. The eldest was studying engineering at Moratuwa University. While in his third year, he was coming home for the holidays. They forced him to get off at Mathavaachchi and hacked him to death, bloody filthy crowd. My daughter is studying BSc at Jaffna University.'

'So you have seen the true nature of the enemy.'

'Is there any Tamil who has not? That is a group born to destroy Tamils. Then the Indian Army came and burned down all that we possessed, just another set of rogues. We can't live in peace as long as they are here,' lamented the old man. Then he asked, 'What is going to happen on the coming Maaveerar Day? Do you think they will try to disrupt it?'

I smiled saying, 'Even if he tries, we are not going to let him.'

'I have not been to Colombo recently. You should have seen their arrogance during 1983 and 1984. They treated Tamils like playthings, to do whatever they liked with. They would force us, young and old, to get off the bus and walk, threaten us, and insult us. Sometimes they would spit on us. They would stop the bus and make us get off in the middle of the forest and leave us there. All the Sinhalese in the bus would be laughing at us. It was a disgusting life for the Tamils. Now they will know what the Tamils are capable of.'

'Iya, I will take my leave now.'

'If you come my way, drop in on us.'

As I was leaving, I turned back to look and saw the old man picking up his spade and walking away. Perhaps there is no Tamil heart that has not been crushed by the enemy.

The moonlight had dimmed. I saw that it was 8.15 p.m. The moon had begun to disappear.

Since all the targets surrounding the enemy camp had been well selected, we prepared to go several kilometres from Maankulam the next morning. The vehicle sped away, tearing through the wind.

'This is the old Kokkaavil camp. We attacked it as soon as the present clashes began. About one hundred army men would have died here. Did you watch the video?' I asked.

'Parts of it are not clear,' Salam said, and kept turning to look at the camp till it disappeared.

'How many days did the attack last?'

'Only two days.'

'On the day the attack started, the army in the camp stopped a bus, stole from the passengers and beat them before they let them go. During 1984 and 1985, their unruly conduct was at its peak. They built the camp saying that it was to protect the TV tower of the State Television. There—that is the junction. Bus drivers, truck drivers, everyone was frightened to pass through it. The army men would climb the trees and wait.'

Only a few days back, this piece of land had been recaptured from the occupier. The remains of the destruction wrought by them were smouldering. The enemy camp was still burning. Now we could roam free. No one would ask why we were going at this time or that. Or who we were and so on. The breeze carried the names of the maaveerars, giving us fresh confidence.

'You know, when the enemy was here, he would force the passengers to get off the vehicle and get back on at Mullaitheevu, Oddusuddaan, Kokkaavil, Kilinochchi, Elephant Pass or Naavatkuli. The passengers would be exhausted. We have started to clear the army occupation little by little,' I told Salam and Ithayan, and we laughed.

5

Battle Preparations

13 November 1990

The vehicle developed a flat tyre after passing Kilinochchi. We changed it and went on. After a long drive we stopped for a break inside a mango orchard. There we changed over to a tractor trailer and continued our journey through a sandy lane. The lane was in a terrible state. Going over huge potholes and water puddles, we got churned inside out. At one spot, there was a forty-foot-wide stream rushing across the lane. The tractor trailer sprayed us with mud and water. We hugged our rifles close, protecting them inside our shirts. After the tractor trailer crossed the rushing water we came upon an open space to our left. It had a few palmyra trees and other trees, and some bushes.

At the far end of that open space, people could be seen like little specks. We sped towards them after identifying ourselves.

'Machan, park the tractor trailer under that tree where it cannot be seen from the air. Helicopters are around, and if the enemy sees us, we will be asking for trouble.'

There were several people there including David annai, Darwin, and Cheeran who had left us earlier.

'Look! Our uncle,' I ran and embraced him.

These pooralis had been with us during special training. We had been together in the battle for Jaffna Fort. We had then left for the Mullaitheevu-camp attack and were now on our way back. They had arrived here after the Fort battle.

'What is this? You have made pouches in blue and have a rifle on your waist,' I teased one of the pooralis.

'Baanu annai gave it to me when the battle for the Fort got over,' said Ranjan.

'If you had told me that you didn't have green material for pouches I would have sent you some,' I joked.

'You don't have to give me any.' Ranjan punched me on my back softly.

He had gained a little weight. He had also turned a little darker. Everyone's hair looked like birds' nests.

'We don't have the time,' Varman said.

Varman had grown up in Colombo and was working when he went back to Jaffna. He was short and lighter skinned. Usually, he would wear his hair very short and neat. Now it was like a basket.

'Yelsin, you look sad,' I teased the one who was half asleep.

'Nothing, I just feel very sleepy.'

This boy can sleep! Varman and him must be in competition for the title of the sleep king. In the mornings, after the wake-up call, they would still be sleeping. Warnings are issued at 7.00, 8.00 and 8.30 a.m. Then they get a bucket of cold water over them before they get out of bed. Both get the cold water bucket at least twice a week.

I pointed to Victor. 'How is sir today?'

Victor approached us, smiling. His curly sideburns had grown and now resembled a beard. Glasses covered his eyes, and his overgrown hair covered his forehead. He too had put on some weight.

'Are you talking about me?'

'I was just asking if you still get a beating from Roy annai.' He gave me a punch in the stomach and I let out a fake cry of pain.

We talked about the pooralis known to all of us in the group. There were many new faces too. I suddenly remembered the one we had nicknamed Number 40. He was called this because he had once applied Number-40 engine oil to his hair and body thinking it was sesame oil. He was there too.

All the poovarasu trees had grown bushy and green with the rain. Yet, the midday sun was making everything burning hot. On one side the pooralis were checking the cannons. We were constantly communicating over the walkie-talkie.

By the time the testing was completed it was 5.30 p.m.

'Quickly, put up two posts here to use as target practice,' Siraj annai told us. Two posts were set up with 125 sandbags by 6 p.m.

Siraj annai started giving orders, as the video cameras whizzed.

'Who is that standing in a sarong? Get down NOW,' he yelled.

Before he finished, Varman joined in. 'Idiot, get down,' he called and pulled the man down.

As Varman raised his voice to scold the man, Siraj annai started to laugh. 'Is that Varathan? He never listens.'

Varathan came down, embarrassed, holding on to his sarong. Siraj annai smiled and everyone applauded; all the while the video cameras kept whirring.

Our weapons were trained upon the fake security-posts. They were blown to pieces. In the darkness, the boom of the artillery echoed, and flashed like lightning. The pieces flew for several hundred metres in all directions.

'Dangerous stuff. Look at all the holes it has dug.'

'The attack on Jaffna Fort was like this. They dropped everything and ran when we started firing. They were really frightened. Later they stayed inside little caves wearing helmets, and just cooked and ate.' Ranjan and Varman described the Fort attack together.

'Have you had a look inside the Fort?'

'Oh yes, we did; twice or thrice.'

'So it is only we who have not seen it. If I survive this attack, I will definitely go there,' I said.

It was very dark now. Because two of our vehicles were stuck in the mud, some of us had to spend the night in the open ground. Food came at 8.30 p.m. Ranjan, Varman, karate-master Alahu and I, opened the parcels and shared the food.

'Master, there are five of us, but there are only two jute sacks to sleep on,' someone complained.

There was a mock quarrel for the sacks. In the end all five of us lay down on the two sacks, without any pillows—straight, like logs.

The sky spread out above with a scattering of stars. A few night birds flew by. The night wind chilled the body. I rolled down my folded shirtsleeves and tried to sleep.

'Ouch. . . . My legs are numb with cold.' This was the Master.

'Yes, yes, it is cold. What can we do?' asked Alahu.

'Is the poor boy feeling cold? Take a shovel and dig a hole. I will bury you and leave your head above; that will keep you warm,' said Master, attempting, in his usual style, to turn hardships into jokes.

'You know that if you belong to the movement you must endure hardships. You must put up with the cold, you must stand in water for hours on end, and sometimes you must go hungry for two or three days. Did you think you could sleep on a mattress under a blanket and drink coffee in bed?'

I laughed, but I could see that Alahu was embarrassed.

Master was talking about the sap from a creeper called thillai. He was telling us that it could burn the skin. Those were the last words I heard before I closed my eyes and fell asleep.

14 November 1990

When we woke up, the early morning dew had settled on all of us. The mist was thick and you could barely see beyond a few metres. We all got up, shivering. Then the morning rays revived our cold bodies, and the dew soon began to disappear. 'No toothpaste, no toothbrush; all of you just come to the river bank to finish the morning chores,' ordered Master.

We finished the morning chores in the river and warmed ourselves with black tea made with the same river water. By 10.30 a.m. we had completed all the testing and started to leave the open space in a crowd. Ranjan, Varman, Ithayan, Alahu and the rest of us made a group of seven and began our planning.

'You go and get Master's rifle,' we urged Alahu.

'Master, give me the rifle; I will hold it.'

Master looked at him suspiciously.

'You said your shoulders were aching. Why don't you give it to me to keep?'

Alahu repeated our suggestion like a parrot. Master looked at Alahu, surprised—unable to believe that his student could care so much about him.

'I do not want to deny your wish. After all, is it not the very last wish?! When you return, it is sure to be in a coffin. I will be the one making the announcement at the funeral parade.'

Saying this, Master began humming a sorrowful tune and then began announcing, in the usual LTTE style, the death of Alahu in the battle of Maankulam.

'Master, come, let us sit in the trailer,' I said, and winked at the others, unnoticed by Master.

'Master, you look very hot,' I said after we all sat in it.

'It was all that sleeping last night, out in the cold dew,' said Master, and continued to spin a yarn in his usual manner.

'Once upon a time there was a king. He wanted to go hunting. He asked his minister whether it would rain that day. The minister said it was a good day to go hunting. On his way to the jungle, the king met a man on the donkey. The man paid his homage to the king and then begged the king not go hunting because it was going to rain. The king ignored him and proceeded.'

At this point Master punched Alahu on his head and said, 'Oh, it is you. I thought it was the man on the donkey.'

Alahu nodded his head behind Master's back, patiently promising himself that his turn for revenge would be coming up soon. Master continued with his story.

'The king was soaked in the rain. He was outraged. He returned to the palace and even before he changed into dry clothes, ordered his guards to bring the man on the donkey.

When the king interrogated the man, he said that he did not know about the rain, but it was the donkey that knew about it. The king then ordered his men . . .'

At this point Master fell from the trailer into a pool of water on the street. He struggled for a second, and then got up and began chasing the tractor. He slipped and fell three times.

We stopped the tractor a bit farther away and asked, 'Did you fall off the trailer, Master?'

'This idiot pushed me! You too, I think!' He began casting aspersions on all of us.

I denied the accusation outright saying he too was a member of our Special Task Force, and gave him a hand to get back on the trailer.

We carried out several such 'operations' that we had up our sleeves. This was our first 'operation' after not being together for many months.

Our units completed the training by 6.30 p.m. and began moving towards Maankulam. The seven of us got into the same tractor trailer. Ithayan had joined us now. This time Master was watchful.

'These fools push people off moving tractors and no doubt think it funny when someone breaks a bone.'

'Will Alahu and Varathan put scorpions down our shirts?' Varman dragged the two into the conversation. The vehicle sped along.

The night was just beginning; the moon was not visible yet. The stars had gathered in clusters looking for the moon in their twinkling light. Clouds cut across the sky frequently.

The destroyed Paranthan homes and school were still visible through the darkness. Once, people lived in this town in contentment. Today, only the occasional light of oil lamps came from tiny huts. The colourful city lights were all gone. The town was silent and sad. Why is this the fate of cities in the Tamil homeland? We will create a sweet new life for them.

'Did you see the state of the town and the school? What harm did they do to him? He just wanted to destroy our places.'

For the first time I saw the anger inside Master. I realized there was a volcano bubbling inside his heart. Pooralis look happy and fun-loving on the surface. But every poorali is a volcano inside—a cool river with a bubbling volcano underneath.

When a poorali is engaged in battle with the enemy, his love for his homeland bursts out like a volcano. Even the enemy is struck with admiration. One Indian military chief who had to deal with us later commented, 'We estimated the manpower of the LTTE, but we failed to estimate their mental and spiritual strength. For that failure we are now paying.' Similar is the assessment of the Tigers by the entire world.

'Machan, go slow near the Kilinochchi camp. We can take a look,' I shouted to Salam.

'This is the old camp. They were chased out only two or three months ago. This tall building housed a police station. The army also occupied part of this building. There is a small lake behind it. This side of the lake was occupied by him.'

'Did he not destroy any of the buildings?' asked Master.

'You will soon see the buildings. He destroyed all the shops and stole all the stock.'

The buildings were in a very bad state. Many were blackened: they had been set alight.

'Over there was the hospital.' A huge building complex stood there, completely destroyed.

'This is the warehouse for paddy. The enemy used this building too. They used to bring the local boys here. Some of the boys have told me what they did to them. What they did is unspeakable. Many boys have died here. Many of the boys could only crawl as their limbs had been broken. It was common to hear women screaming inside these buildings. Later, the bodies were dragged to vehicles, taken to the forest and burned,' I repeated what my friends, who were first-hand witnesses, told me.

'One day . . .'

'Stop. . . . I can't listen to this any more.' Master's hand shook me, forcing me to stop. I sensed the anger and the conviction in those shaking hands.

'Machan, two of my very close friends disappeared like this. Not even their ashes were handed over to their families. These are cowards who show their bravery by attacking innocent, unarmed people.'

Two warm teardrops fell on my arm. I looked up at the sky. The moon had begun to climb. Master gazed in the direction of an elephant trumpeting. The barrel of the AK-47 [assault rifle], resting on the knee and held firmly in the hand, could be seen moving with the swaying of the vehicle. This was a day we were all touched by strong emotions.

Some of our units stopped at Maankulam. Three units needed to move to the other side of the Maankulam camp. In order to reach a location just forty metres away, we travelled nearly forty kilometres. Around 1 a.m. we woke up by a tea shop in Oddusuddaan and had tea. Each of us drank large mugs of tea.

Hunger and the cold made our journey hard. After tea we continued our journey towards Kanakaraayankulam.

We all started to doze off. Each of us leaned on the person next to us, all the while trying to sleep sitting upright. The regular shaking of the tractor trailer frequently woke us and we yelled at Salam in unison. Salam just laughed as he continued his driving. He too dozed off sometimes while driving, but his driving did not allow us to sleep for five minutes, undisturbed.

Thick forests ran on either side as we drove. The moon was above our heads now. We all woke up as the tractor trailer came to a sudden stop.

'Machan, look there. What a huge snake!'

We all looked. In the tractor's headlight, something brown was glistening. It was at least fifteen centimetres in diameter, and six metres long.

'Is it a python?' queried Master.

At everyone's urging, Salam drove the tractor wheel over the python's head. Suddenly everyone in the trailer screamed.

The six-metre python had swung its tail and hit the trailer. The python continued to hit the trailer several times. We all peered over the side of the tractor to look at the python. A bloodied white rabbit came out of its mouth. A few baby rabbits scurried away, probably looking for their mother. The python set its teeth on the tyre of the tractor and froze. The baby rabbits continued to search for their mother.

The struggle of life goes on everywhere. Loss, too, occurs everywhere. That day the cow's calf was taken by a crocodile.

A mongoose kills a peacock. The peacock rips a snake. The alkaaddi, that warns everyone, also loses its eggs to something in the fields. The mother rabbit is swallowed by the python and baby rabbits search for their mother. This is the struggle for food among all living beings.

Humans are different. Of course they have to show that they are above all other living beings. Humans kill their own kind, not for food, but to dominate. To wipe out those who kill to dominate is a far greater deed than to kill a crocodile or a python. The one who kills those who kill to dominate, and thus gives protection to the innocent, is an enlightened soul.

6

The Battle Is On

15 November 1990

Around 5.10 a.m., still enveloped by fog, we hurriedly parked the tractor trailer among the tall bushes and walked towards a hut to wash our faces. The darkness melted, but the fog remained. On the left side of the road, set slightly farther back, was another little hut.

'There is no point calling from outside the gate. Let's go inside,' suggested Ranjan.

We removed the sticks blocking the gate's entrance and began walking into the yard.

On both sides of the footpath, yellow and red flowers were in full bloom. The marigold must have just bloomed. The petals were moist and smooth. A large neem tree in the corner gave plenty of shade. A tiny shrine stood at the base of the tree.

'Amma, can we wash our faces in your well?'

'Yes, come this way.'

'Take some toothpaste, and go and wash,' the amma said.

Near the well the vegetable plot was lush and green. The plants were weighed down by the vegetables.

'How do you water these plants, amma? Kerosene for the water pump is expensive, isn't it?' I asked.

'Who needs kerosene? We can water with the thula. Our son helps with it. It takes maybe two hours to water all these plants.'

Her son, standing nearby, was only nine years old. I thought to myself that in Jaffna it was so very different. The children there would still be in bed or would have gone to tuition classes.

Today we depend so much on the food-ships and trucks bringing foreign food to us. When will our own self-sufficient economy that was destroyed by colonialism come up again? Our economy will only grow when our people become aware of what has been done to us.

'Thambi, all of you, come and have tea.'

'No, no, we will drink here.'

'No, no, it is okay. Come in and have tea.'

The cups in which the tea was served were modest, but the tea itself, with fresh cow's milk, tasted superb. We were all energized.

We said goodbye and got on the road. We walked along and found a log to sit on. A monkey sat on a tree across the road and stared.

'Look at my grandpa,' said Master and threw a stone at it. The monkey leaped off.

We ate the bread and bananas brought to us by Mani annai and discussed how we needed sleep.

'Where will you be at noon?' Mani annai asked.

'We will eat and sleep. We will not be going anywhere,' we said.

'I am leaving now. There are buns and biscuits in the tin.'

'Okay, annai, see you.'

As soon as Mani annai's head disappeared, everyone jumped on the bag.

'Leave it, boys. I will distribute the food,' said Master, and he did.

The breeze was wonderful. We were able to sleep well. We tidied the ground, removing the leaves, and spread sacks and lay down. In the afternoon we went for a walk through the paddy fields. We reached a mango orchard and a Lankan government office where not a soul was to be seen anywhere. We picked a variety of mangoes and sat down by a water canal and started to eat. Two peacocks in the fields ran away when one of us stood up and shouted.

We started off at night and arrived at the Maankulam camp early in the morning and quietly stayed put. From now on, it was of absolute importance for us to maintain secrecy. Even if our own people saw us, it was possible that the military would be alerted and our plans wrecked. For this reason we strengthened the security lines around us. We stayed where we were until the next day. Then we walked to the camp to do some preparatory work.

16 November 1990

On 16th morning, at 9 a.m., we reached our security-posts. We sent off Varman to his post on the other side of the camp.

'Master, look. Let us stay in this house,' I said.

We went inside the house. It was the same one, with the outer walls destroyed, that I had seen when I came here the first time.

'Master, it is your job to control the boys. They will not follow my orders,' I said.

'Don't try to trick me again.'

'I promise,' and I proceeded to put my hand on his head to show that the promise was real.

He checked my hand saying, 'Okay, okay, go away. I will handle the boys. The boys will not obey you, for such is your ugly face!'

'Okay, I will go to my post.'

I jumped over the barrier. I stopped to chat with the other pooralis at the security-posts, and returned to the house. Master and Alahu were tidying the house.

'Alahu, machan, when did you come?'

'This prince arrived just now. The idiot got into the wrong tractor, went off to the other side of the camp,' Master laughed aloud.

'Hey! It was you who pushed me into the water, was it not?'

I read the situation quickly and realized I would be given a cold shower if I went near him. I invited them into the house while standing far away from them. Then I went inside and sat on the veranda.

Master called, 'Alahu, can you go in and get the biscuits . . .'

Before he could finish, I rushed in to beat Alahu to the biscuits. As I opened the door, a bucket of water tied to the door tipped over, drenching me.

Master and Alahu's loud laughter could be heard as I walked towards the well with a defeated smile.

When we all lay down for a rest, Master asked me to tell him about Kannan, another poorali we knew, and how he died.

Kannan had been driving the tractor. He was terribly

sleepy and was dozing off. I kept tapping his shoulder to wake him up. He yelled at me for constantly tapping him. After a while, the tractor's course changed and it felt like we were going over a log. I couldn't see Kannan in front. I stopped the tractor, got off and saw that the log was actually Kannan. The tractor had gone over his chest.

I fell asleep thinking about Kannan. He was a good weapon-maker. He joined the movement despite being the son of a big businessman and having the privileges that went with it.

22 November 1990

The twenty-second arrived as we laughed, joked and worked. The morning was not that cold. The sun was up early too. Birds were busy singing and hopping about the trees. Peacocks came down from the treetops to the fields. They pecked at the grains on the ground. Parrots in big flocks landed on the fruit creepers densely growing there. Monkeys sat on trees and watched us intently.

The gentle breeze embraced us all. Unwilling to leave the pooralis, the breeze banged its head on the walls of the security-posts. The clouds rushed by, shedding some tears and wiping their eyes. That sweet morning was bidding us pooralis farewell. Birds sang mournfully and left. A cock could be heard far away. We sat together for a cup of tea and began our preparations.

Master came and sat by me.

'What is it, Master? What is that look about?'

'I just wanted to have a good look at you before letting you go.'

'You bastard,' I started to chase him.

We had lunch together under the tree.

The usually hot rays of the sun spread their gentle heat on us. The poovarasu trees that droop in the heat were standing upright. The breeze surrounded the pooralis and brought with it flower petals from the poovarasu. The hut was cool and cosy. Even the crows crowed more pleasantly, inviting their kin.

'If the crow crows while flying, a letter will arrive. If it crows while walking, a visitor will arrive,' said Master.

'What if it sits down and crows?' I asked.

'Artillery shells will arrive,' he said.

We hurried to our meeting.

A large group of pooralis were sitting in rows. They were firmly holding various types of weapons in their hands. Their faces were bright, intent and full of conviction.

On one side stood female pooralis. They were the burning lights rising from a male-dominated society. They represented the historic steps into the future.

A lieutenant in the front expressed his opinion on the Maankulam camp. 'This camp was set up in 1971 to suppress the uprising among the Sinhala youth. It was re-established in 1978, and has remained a huge hurdle to our movement. It has been a source of disruption of normalcy in people's lives. It is a cruel camp that is destroying the resources of Tamil Eelam; it is a threat to our environment. We have attacked this camp once, but it was not a complete success. We must make up for the shortcomings in that attack.'

Our discussion went on to many more topics and got over only at 4.30 p.m. We returned to our posts and started getting ready. Around 5 p.m. two Y-12 planes [multipurpose aircrafts modified and used as bombers by the Sri Lankan Air Force] flew in from the south.

'Machan, do you think he has been alerted?' asked Master, firmly holding on to his weapons.

'Let us wait and see. They may be coming to drop off food,' I consoled him.

The two planes separated and started flying in big circles.

'Master, get the boys to transfer the shells into the bunker,' I said.

I could see him rushing off. Ithayan, with walkie-talkie in hand, could be seen nearby. Darwin was walking away with Master. Ranjan was squatting under a tree.

'Did he drop something?' Ranjan asked.

'Oh, he has dropped it.'

As all three of us watched, it came down with a hissing sound and hit the ground with a thud far away from the camp. Perhaps near the school.

'It is the thing. It is all going awry,' said Master standing near a tree.

The other plane cut in and made a smaller circle.

'It's a bomb, look. It is coming down like a shuttlecock. All take cover!' As Ithayan said this, we could see the bomb going past us. We straightened up from our crouching positions.

Following the loud noise of the exploding bombs there was non-stop gunfire from the army camp.

'Do you think he has been alerted?' asked someone, in a state of shock. As he said this, a bullet hit a tree nearby.

'Is there a problem?' the leader asked through the walkie-talkie.

'No problem,' said another voice from the walkie-talkie.

Another plane circled round and round and dropped four parcels. One fell behind me. The next one was dropped in front of us, just opposite the previous one.

'Machan, this one is near us. All take cover,' I shouted and everyone scrambled to take cover.

It came down with a loud hissing noise and exploded with a frightening sound. The sand on the side of the bunker fell off with the shock.

We all came out brushing the sand from our heads. The small hut where we were staying had disappeared without a trace. Near where it had been was a huge crater in the ground. The planes had disappeared into the distance. We could now hear a howl of pain. We all walked over to where it was coming from. The dog that we had fed for the last four days was lying on the ground, minus a leg, and with a big wound.

'Master, look at our dog,' said Alahu.

'The poor fool. Now, now, don't start playing the dog-owner; go on and do your work.'

The dog looked at us pathetically.

'Okay, come and bring out all the shells.'

It was 6.05 p.m. The sun was turning red in the western sky. The sky, the clouds and everything else in the sky were brushed with patches of red. Perhaps they were crying over the blood that was about to flow. Birds were hurrying back to their nests. The flapping of their wings conveyed sadness. Animals howled. Of all the sounds, the howl of the dog gradually pervaded every place and thing, and then eventually died down. A lonely lost heron flew past. In patches, there were flocks of bats in flight. My heart was shaken by the sad songs of two alkaaddi birds that first circled us, then the enemy camp, and then flew away. The sun had now descended into the earth. The clouds too had fled. The time was 6.35 p.m.

'Machan, is everything set up okay? Come over here. The shells and rounds will soon be flying and you are standing there without any cover. Be careful,' I warned those standing around.

The mouth of the cannon, camouflaged by tree branches, was aimed at the police station.

It was now 6.56 p.m.

'Who is approaching?' I said sharply.

'It is me, Master.' He took a pair of pliers and ran back.

6.58 p.m. . . .

'Ranjan, is everything okay?' I wiped my face with the back of my hand. The walkie-talkie started and a red light shone.

7 p.m. . . .

'Okay, go,' the leader ordered and the firing of the projectiles shook the enemy camp before the guns there started to operate. The entire earth appeared to be shaking.

The noise from the camp was loud. It was the cry of the enemy dying. Enemy fire began to reach everywhere. We faced the heaviest fire because we were very close to the enemy camp. Bullets hit tree trunks and branches, and exploded.

Various types of bullets, some of them very powerful, were all coming our way. Some of them passed between our legs. Yet, in the life-or-death battle, we sent a constant barrage of bullets, and the confused enemy fired in the wrong direction. Bullets went over trees and even towards the sky.

'Look, from that post in the shop he is firing 30 calibres.'

Shells could be seen flying from that post in other directions. The shop had caught fire from our attack. The ammunitions inside the shop had started to explode.

Every second, we received commands through the walkie-talkie about the mode and direction of our attack. We followed the orders. Gradually the number of pooralis began to diminish as they were wounded and removed from the battleground. Those of us remaining continued with our attack.

Suddenly there were bullets coming straight down, and they hit the trees. Only then did we see the two helicopters. They started firing into our positions.

Five-inch shells and RPG shells rained down, and many guns started firing at us. We decided to take the plunge and attacked one target from three angles simultaneously. Our target, the police station, collapsed under our fire.

We would have faced many losses if we had not adopted this strategy. Suddenly there were two huge bangs and my eardrums almost burst. I felt the blood oozing from my leg. It was a minor injury. Only later did I realize that it was an aerial bombing raid by the enemy.

We continued with our fast attack when another bomber came. Our 50-mm calibres were aimed at it and they started to spit shells. The bomber rose and backed away. Amidst the noise of the 50 mm-calibre fire we heard cries of pain. There was a problem at Cheeran's post. I ordered the others to continue the attack and ran there. Four young pooralis were lying in a pool of blood. Master arrived from the next post.

'Take the boys away from there. He will hit again at that range.'

Carrying the young pooralis we moved back. Soon the boom was heard again.

'Is there a problem, Master?'

'No, no, it's just a bruised hand. Walk fast.'

We had already informed the medics via walkie-talkie about the four young pooralis. The medic-pooralis started first aid without delay. One of the four young pooralis, injured in the stomach, was lying in my arms. He grabbed my hand and tightened his grip. It felt as if he was using every bit of life left in him to grip me. His voice too came out using all the energy left in him.

'Machan, invade the camp, kill them all, and grab every bit of equipment that you can.'

His young life dissolved in the breeze and entered my heart and filled the space around. His grip loosened. A star fell, leaving its silvery trail. The last words of the young poorali echoed in my ears among all the outside noises.

We hurried back to the battleground. The bushes and forest trees were burning, hit by the shells and bombs. As we rushed back to our locations the shells and bombs continued to fall.

It was 10.15 p.m.

I briefed everyone about what had happened and readied the cannons. I started to monitor our target. Two shells from the enemy flew past us and exploded. Following the order from our leader we aimed our shells in the direction of the enemy.

'Machan, it missed. Before he comes out of the bunker we should fire again.'

Next time, our shell hit the target and we could see the building crashing down. We sent an occasional 'light bomb' to identify our targets, and continued with our attack.

The next shell from the enemy hit a tree and Darwin's thighs began to bleed. I took out the cotton from the field compress in my pocket and applied a pressure bandage. The blood oozed through the bandage.

'It's okay, buddy. Set up the next one' said Darwin.

'Are you mad? You have shrapnel inside your thigh. You can't stay here with blood pouring out like this.' I got mad, but he was adamant that he would stay on.

The warmongers who are occupying our land are mercenaries working for wages. If their life is threatened during battles, they hide somewhere and indiscriminately open fire. They will back out of battle at the slightest injury. Our pooralis are very different. They dedicate their life and body to the battlefield. They value a free homeland more than their life. They never back away from a battle. They refuse to leave the battleground even if badly injured. They leave only as lifeless bodies or if removed by others when they lose the ability to function. This is the quality of our pooralis. It is this quality that paves the way for victories over the arrogant occupier, full of confidence.

We continued with our attack. We had damaged their long-distance communication system, and as a result one of their helicopters fired into their own camp. We stayed where we were, facing stiff attacks from the air and the enemy camp.

A plane began to circle overhead. We took cover immediately. A bomb fell just fifty metres away and a huge paalai tree was reduced to smithereens. Pieces of the tree struck us and bruised our skin. Our attack was complete when we took aim at the bank building.

11.59 p.m. The cannons boomed for the final fire, shook the camp and went quiet.

12 a.m., midnight. Firmly holding on to their weapons, our pooralis started to crawl through the darkness. The night silently bid them goodbye. Only the helicopters in the sky broke the darkness.

The grass gently caressed their crawling bodies. It bent over, trying to make their path soft. There was no moonlight. The clouds hid the stars, keeping the darkness as we crawled past the open paddy fields. With the enemy stunned by our fire, we crawled forward to destroy them completely and recover our land.

It was the enemy fire that started first, thus launching the face-to-face attacks. The fire from the enemy camp intensified as our pooralis, sculptors of the future, crawled on with no cover. Finally our guns began to show the enemy the ground truth. Enemy fire began falling in the open plain, like raindrops. Helicopters, too, began their hunt for their prey in the paddy fields.

The helicopters were spitting 50-mm calibres non-stop. Our ground fire chased them back up to the clouds. Our brave pooralis were floating in a river of blood. Tiger-soldiers jumped over enemy bodies to combat more army men. The enemy camp fell apart due to our RPG fire, and the mercenary force started to run away.

I turned the walkie-talkie on and our leader's orders came non-stop. Jegan annai and Vathanan annai were constantly being called over the walkie-talkie among the regular orders being issued. Soon Thileepan annai's and Gopu's names were also called on the walkie-talkie several times. Their connection was broken. They were moving forward to capture the camp at the nuns' hostel. I thought something must be wrong. It is very unusual for all the leaders of the four divisions to be moving towards a target to be cut off.

Yet, a little later, another voice announced that they had captured some of the positions near that same hostel. Our leader congratulated them and promised to send reinforcements.

I was able to work out that a battle was going on near the temple and our pooralis were getting closer. Injured pooralis began to arrive from the division that approached the police station. I went behind, along the railway track. Bullets were whizzing around. I heard the groan of a wounded poorali. A poorali, hit in the stomach, was lying there, unable to move. I gave him a shoulder and took him with me. I could see bullets hitting the railway track in a line.

My hands searched the poorali's neck looking for his cyanide capsule. The practice in the LTTE is to remove the cyanide capsule from an injured poorali's neck, to prevent them from biting the capsule while suffering pain. He grabbed my hand very tight.

'I am not going to die so quickly without chasing away those bastards. If I can't today, I will come back tomorrow.'

He said this, gritting his teeth in anger. He did not appear to be someone crying because of the pain in his body. His thoughts were entirely on the battleground. Continuing to grip my hands, he told me, 'Leave the rifle "on safety",' and fainted.

I changed the lever on the rifle and handed it to another poorali, and moved forward, fast. Shells narrowly missed me as I crouched and ran towards the gunfire of our division.

'Machan, there are two injured pooralis and no one to carry them; hurry up and take them,' ordered a poorali.

I slung the rifle again on my shoulder and moved, crouching, towards the house where the enemy was stationed. Two pooralis lay there, having lost a lot of blood. There were no bandages at hand. Where can one go looking for bandages when shells are constantly whizzing past. I took off my tiger-striped shirt and cut it up with a knife. I tied a bandage around the wounded stomach of one poorali. His breathing was slowing down. The other poorali had an apple-sized hole in his thigh. I wrapped that too.

Giving the pooralis a shoulder each and hiding behind any available cover, I started moving back.

The one injured in the stomach kept trying to shout. 'Give him one, machan, and keep on moving inside.'

But his shout came out in a soft, pained tone. His hand folded over the rifle-sling, making it impossible for me to remove the rifle from him. His voice slowly grew softer. I could now see a figure coming towards us.

'Hand one over to me; it is hard to carry them both.'

'Master? I will carry them both. You go to the front and bring someone.'

'Leo. Take them to the medics in the bunker near the tree.' I could see him running fast.

I handed over the two injured pooralis to the medics for treatment. As I turned to go I could see medic-pooralis in large numbers.

'No problem now. Bring any injured poorali here immediately,' said the one in front as he ran, followed by the others.

I waited near the tree for Master. The battle was intense.

I could work out from the messages over the walkie-talkie that the enemy was being weakened and that our divisions were capturing enemy-posts.

'Master, come. If we go to the post at the roadside, we can go join the standby group. If not, we can at least go to the supply group.'

Both of us moved fast. Shells were exploding near us.

'We can capture half the camp today. Guarding the captured area from aerial bombardments will be very difficult,' Master said as he came towards me.

7

A Black Tiger Attack

23 November 1990

The camp surroundings were captured by our pooralis around 4 a.m. after very heavy fighting. Despite exhaustion and thirst, they were all busy building fortifications, to be ready for the aerial attacks that would come with the dawn.

Everyone was fully occupied as they hurriedly dug trenches and put up the sandbags. There was no compulsion from outside for them to work like this. They all worked of their own will. The enemy fire tried in vain to disrupt their work.

The people of Tamil Eelam ought to reflect on this situation. When we request our people for assistance to build bunkers or dig trenches, many parents will not send their children to help.

Following battles, they will mull over newspaper reports, express their opinion, and within minutes return to their own selfish lives.

They fail to empathize with the young pooralis, the same age as their children, battling without food or water. They imagine that the weapons are fighting the battles on their own. They do not see that in the battleground, the pooralis' hearts and minds are also in the fighting. The attitude of some parents saddens and disappoints us, and it can even get to the point where it affects our resolve.

The preparation for the Maankulam battle and other battles is exhausting, and can take days. Most of the work must be done at night. We have to set up new machine-gun positions without the enemy noticing. The sandbags and wood must be carried by us staying low on the ground or even crawling on our knees. It is hard work. The next day we will be so stiff that we have trouble walking straight. Yet, we do it all again on the next day too. Our eyes will be heavy due to the lack of sleep, yet the enemy targets have to be located in daylight. Hunger, while awake at nights, is not new even to civilians. On cold frosty nights we will be soaked. Our throats will be dry and our lips, cracked and paining. It is no trivial matter to wage battles under such conditions and then start building security positions before dawn without even a drink of water.

Pooralis enhance their mental strength through these experiences. These hardships do not affect our conviction. But when we meet an unpatriotic civilian our hearts become heavy. On the other hand when we meet those who are patriotic it strengthens a poorali's conviction and the yearning for freedom burns within us even more intensely.

5 a.m. Two planes and two helicopters began circling the camp. The pooralis could not finish making the bunkers in an hour although they tried hard. Water kept springing from the ground since there had been heavy rain.

The sandbags were also soaked. Then the enemy started simultaneous aerial and land attacks.

The nuns' hostel and the temple came under intense bombardment. We struggled to cope. We were forced to retreat when attacks from the land started. One of the positions we retreated from was the temple area.

They started repairing the security-post that they had recaptured from us. This rebuilding activity boded danger. We realized that when the enemy relaunched attacks from the rebuilt positions we would have to lose many more of our pooralis to take the post back. There was also the psychological boost they would gain by restoring security-posts of theirs that we had destroyed.

We therefore launched a very risky and daring operation, moving forward through the open fields in broad daylight. The enemy did not expect this. For a moment he was disoriented by the sudden attack. The enemy soon realized that he was facing the final blow to his station. Moving through the open space, he began firing at us. Bombers rained missiles on us.

Fallen pooralis and their fresh blood, rather than young green paddy, now covered the fields of Maankulam, one of the richest granaries of Tamil Eelam. Even in their final moments, the pooralis enriched the land they loved. These young pooralis who longed to breathe free air and put their footprints on their homeland now dissolved into the breeze over the fields. Their friends who were with them, who were reborn in the same training camps, who laughed and played together, continued to move forward towards the enemy. These brave, fallen heroes, even in death, did not find a human hand to comfort them. They are the saints who gave up the joys of youth for the freedom they so dearly loved.

The enemy, unable to cope with the losses, began to give up the security-posts one by one. We recaptured each one. In that sweet afternoon, at 4 p.m., we captured the post near the temple on the Electricity Road.

The pooralis, relentless, gladly consumed the gentle breeze as food. The enemy was now restricted to his main camp. We could see very clearly that he was now shaky.

It is in times like this that we request our people to give us dry food. If we are to move into the camps captured at night, it can only be in the morning. When our people happily give us dry food with the feeling that it is for 'our boys', the food tastes delicious. It gives us an energy that is refreshing.

When we eat we see the smiling faces of the mothers whom we have met during our struggle. It gives us profound satisfaction.

The evening of the 23rd melted away, longing for something. The sun was a flaming red. There were no sweet songs of birds. They had kept away today, but tomorrow they would welcome the morning with their melodies. The songs would gently caress the headstones of the saintly souls. Today they had disappeared into the forest. The blanket of night fell over everything.

24 November 1990

We left Kanakaraayankulam early, at 6 a.m., to launch our attack with fewer mortars than we used yesterday. People were waiting for us in large numbers at the junction. They stopped us, gave us snacks, and wished us well. As our vehicle started to move, the poorali at the back shouted something. We stopped the vehicle and looked behind. A grand old lady in a pure white sari was walking hurriedly towards us. She was holding a home-made bag. We all got off and ran towards her.

'What is the matter, aachchi?'

'I was walking. When I saw you leaving I had to run. All of you come here.'

She took out the holy ash, wrapped in a leaf, from her bag and put it on our foreheads, and gave us all a kiss on our cheeks.

Holy ash has a great religious significance among Hindu Tamils. Although the LTTE is a secular movement, people use their own rituals to show their love and respect for the pooralis.

Our tiredness after the battle disappeared. A new rush of energy entered us. The grief of losing our comrades disappeared in that moment. Our heavy hearts melted at her touch.

'You must fight well and come back victorious. I will be waiting in that hut.'

These were words from a mother of Tamil Eelam. Her voice broke as she uttered them. We all felt blessed to hear these words.

'We will, for sure, kill them all and capture our land,' a poorali said with obvious emotion.

She took sweet rice from her bag and put some in our mouths. It gave us renewed energy.

This patriotic mother had given us a kind of joy that we would not get from great victories on the battleground. She stood there, watching us until we disappeared. Tears slid down my cheeks. We will not stop on our path as long as there are mothers like this. Master, sitting next to me, stared in her direction. I could see the joy on his face too. He hummed a tune, the words of which were 'We are going towards the enemy camp.'

We saw red dots passing above us in a row.

'Machan, stop! The helicopters are firing.'

The vehicle's lights were switched off and it was parked under a tree. The helicopter went round and kept firing. Red bullets struck the tar road and rebounded. We all got into the water canal running along the side of the road.

'He is only ploughing the road,' someone said.

Again bullets hit the road in a line. We could work out from the noise that two bullets had hit our tractor and the cannon gun.

There was a loud hissing noise.

'All take cover. He has fired 5-inch calibres.'

Two shells exploded in the rice fields nearby.

It was now 7.35 p.m.

'We can't wait any more. Let him keep firing. Ithayan, take the tractor.'

As soon as the order was given, Ithayan ran without hesitation towards the tractor trailer. The rest of us started running on both sides of the road. The helicopter chased us, firing all the while.

'He is flying over our heads. He could drop something big any time. Watch out.'

Barely had these words been uttered, when shells started coming. One exploded just a hundred metres behind us on the road. We kept running, exploiting the explosion, using it as cover. The helicopter came back over the centre of the road. On high alert, we took cover as 50-mm-calibre shells pounded the road, making huge potholes. We could see Ithayan turning towards the security-post. We ran through the rice fields, bushes and open spaces, and past the railway tracks. Helicopters continued to chase us. Suddenly there was a roaring noise from a helicopter. Two rockets hit a tree and exploded, tearing it apart into pieces. I heard a groan from Master, but he kept running.

I could not ask Master what had happened; the shells kept coming. I reached Master and saw a piece lodged in his arm. I pulled it out and applied a pressure bandage. We were now at our post.

The time was exactly 8.02 p.m. We began emptying our mortars.

The enemy responded with bullets. The intensity of the reaction was far less than on the previous day. He used his ammunition sparingly. Helicopters and aerial bombers, however, gave us more trouble today than yesterday. Our main targets today were his main camp and the rice-warehouse camp. We escaped very narrowly today. One of his bombs fell just ten metres away from us, but it failed to explode. The enemy was unlucky. We removed the unexploded bomb, left it where it would not be set off by our own cannon fire and built a secure post around it. As we did this, helicopters kept firing, trying to finish us off.

On this day, two of our pooralis were injured in the enemy RPG fire. We handed over both of them to our medic-pooralis and hurried on with our attacks.

25 November 1990

12.45 a.m. We sent off our final shell towards the main camp. Two bombers were still circling above us.

It was now 12.59 a.m. Our leader ordered us to silence our cannons and take cover. A large truck loudly drove through the enemy security-posts on the road.

'All of you jump away and watch the truck,' I shouted and took cover.

There was immense light for a second. The wind convulsed and then pushed everything. The noise, the indescribable noise, split the eardrums. The forest trees shook once and slowly became still. Animals stood stumped, in a state of shock. Sulphur smoke blocked our noses.

A hero, a Black Tiger, had made history.

Bork annai!

I remembered meeting Bork annai four days ago. He was relaxing in an easy chair. He had just returned from a visit home and had brought some snacks for us. He was smiling.

'Do your shells make loud noises? I won't come anywhere near them.' He acted as if he was scared.

How would he have bid farewell to his mother. My heart choked as I remembered the gist of a poem written by Bengali Nobel Laureate, Tagore.

'Mother, it is for you. The time has come for me to go. Farewell, mother. When you stretch out your arms, in the quiet darkness of dawn, thinking that your baby who slept next to you is there, I will no longer be there. When you are lying without sleep, I will be among the stars telling you to go to sleep. When the lightning flash passes through your open window, my laughter will come with it. I will come to your bedside with the moonlight and rest my head. I will come as gentle waves of wind and embrace you. I will enter through your eyelids as a dream and go to the depth of your sleep. When you wake up, I will turn into a tiny light and disappear into the darkness. When neighbourhood children are playing in our house, I will come with the music of the flute and fill your heart. When aunty next door comes and asks you for your baby, tell her that your baby is in your eyes and he fills your entire being.'

Would Bork have said all this to his mother?

8

Onward Journey

The night was coming to an end.

Our divisions entered the enemy camps and launched attacks. Since there were no counter-attacks, suspecting the enemy might be waiting in silence, we moved cautiously. We saw the bodies of enemy-soldiers lying scattered. Some of the buildings were on fire.

25 November 1990

By 3 a.m. we had done a thorough search of the enemy camps. Weapons and bodies were scattered everywhere. We collected the weapons. It seemed that the enemy had abandoned the camp and withdrawn into the forest along the Luxabana electricity-towers line. He had moved towards their other camp on the hill. We decided not to follow him immediately as it was still dark.

The next morning we learnt via walkie-talkie that our pooralis had intercepted the withdrawing enemy-soldiers near

Kanakaraayankulam and were attacking them. We could see two helicopters circling that part of the forest.

At 6.15 a.m. we were on our way to the enemy camps to conduct recovery operations. We were moving along the main road on the Vavuniya side. We kept to the road because the enemy had planted landmines all along its sides. Once we moved past our own security-post into the area that had been in the enemy's hands until now, we all sensed the excitement rising within us.

The buildings, mango orchards, coconut estates, all of these were getting nearer. Until now we had watched them, hiding behind trees and walls, and longed to have them. Now they were ours. We could not resist running towards them.

Enemy-posts, flattened and burning, welcomed us. A large tree destroyed by our shells had fallen across the road and was blocking it. The occasional fire was still roaring. I peeped into a post that had been gutted. The bodies of three enemy-soldiers had been burned down to their bones. Their T-58 guns had also got burned; only the iron parts were left behind.

'You left me behind!' Master came running excitedly towards us.

'We called you, but you had gone somewhere to eat,' said Alahu. Master let out a barrage of accusations at Alahu.

'Come here. This is the post we destroyed day before yesterday.'

Alahu came running to see.

'Look, the rifles have all got burned. Bring me a stick and let us see if we can recover any of them.'

'It is useless. The barrels are all bent from the heat,' I said as I picked one up and dropped it on the ground.

'Look there,' Master pointed to the enemy's possessions: his bags, hats, and the clothes drying on the line.

'It looks like quite a number of men were stationed here. Let's go behind the shop and look at the well.'

'Machan!'

I saw the bodies of our pooralis. Two bodies, one obviously killed while dragging the other, were there. Tears welled up in my eyes. Master was staring at the bodies.

'They must have died the day before yesterday.'

'Yes. The poorali had come right inside to rescue the other.'

We told the others over the walkie-talkie and went closer to look.

The first poorali had taken the blast on his chest and stomach.

The one who had come to rescue him had a hole on the left side of his forehead.

'Machan, do not move the bodies in a haste. They may have placed a release switch under the bodies.'

Bombs can be triggered by a release switch, placed under a heavy object. They will go off when the object is removed.

We carefully inspected the two bodies, lifted them and placed them inside the shop. We observed several stab wounds on their bodies caused by a bayonet blade.

'See what they have done to the bodies of our pooralis. They have shown their brutality.' Master stared at the bodies. His anger was very apparent.

The stomach of the poorali with a gunshot wound on his forehead had been slashed in a criss-cross pattern. The body of the other poorali was riddled with marks from a number of bullets.

Even if clashes on the battleground are intense, no soldier will harm the dead body of the enemy-soldier. It is considered the duty of the battling sides to bury the bodies of enemy-soldiers with respect. This custom has existed throughout the ages and throughout the world.

Sinhala chauvinists do not practice this. They rip the dead bodies of pooralis when faced with losses or defeat. It is not hard to imagine the cruelty let loose by these chauvinists upon the civilian population on entering their areas. They are unable to relieve themselves of this mindset.

In this respect they are very different from the pooralis. Pooralis are created when the oppressor's tactics become too brutal. None of the oppressors learn this truth till the end. Even if they do know, they behave as if they do not. They still manage to get some satisfaction by ripping up the dead bodies of pooralis.

We covered the bodies of the pooralis and went towards the well. The clothes on the line were scattered. Many of them were splattered with blood. We went to the well which had a large diameter. The skirting of the well was not high enough and looked dangerous. We passed the well and entered the mango orchard. A huge number of mangoes had fallen on the ground. Some of the mango trees had been damaged too.

'Leo, look at these empty rounds.'

'Oh, they must have used them while withdrawing.' I pointed to the security wall made of railway sleepers. Since they were protecting the enemy from our 50-mm-calibre fire, the bushes in front were burned. This burned mark stretched all way to the enemy-post on the hill.

'Look at these bloodstained clothes.'

'Look, there are a lot there.'

'Quite a few have been wounded or killed.'

We collected the scattered bullets into a pile. Grenades, guns, and shells, too, were found in large numbers.

We put them all in one place. We placed the ammunition that appeared unsafe under a tree and placed a warning sign near it.

The enemy does not really care much about his weapons. There were large amounts of various types of ammunition buried in the sand in places from which he had withdrawn. Pooralis struggled to collect them. They had to put in a lot of effort to dig them out carefully. They moved huge broken pillars in order to reach the ammunition underneath. These were pooralis who had not eaten since noon the previous day, who had been fighting intense battles all night.

I would like to tell our people something about this. The enemy is stronger than us in numbers and weaponry. Our strength is in our determination, belief in our goal, and our love for the land and our people. This is the protective armour we wear as we enter the open space without cover, into enemy camps, camps that are well equipped with weaponry. Our people must keep this in mind. Also, all the ammunition and weapons we capture from the enemy is going to be used by us to attack him tomorrow. Think about it. Each bullet we collect will be used to reduce his numbers. Think about the pooralis who died trying to recover the enemy's weapons. This is why we work hard to collect the ammunition. Through it, we become stronger.

'Master, come, let's go to the big camp.'

As we walked along the road, I reminisced about my younger days here to Master.

'What happened then?' he asked.

'Oh, nothing happened. During 1983 and 1984, we built a new home in Maankulam. In those days, the Mullaitheevu bus would stop at the junction. After we got off there, none of the buses going past Maankulam would pick us up because they were all long-distance buses. So we had to walk home from the junction. Sometimes a lorry would pick us up. It was mostly my mother and I who would be walking. One day, two boys were coming towards us on a bicycle. Two army men came out. We were just ten metres away from them. The army men did not even ask the two boys to stop. They just kicked the boy who was cycling and both boys fell down. They beat the boys brutally with their guns and then dragged them into the camp. The two boys were screaming in pain. We ran away, not looking behind.'

'What happened then?'

'We do not know. Someone said that their bodies were left in the hospital by the army who said they had been killed by elephants in the forest.'

'Military Camp—Maankulam', the bloodstained board written in Sinhala stood on top of the cement wall. This is the place where those fanatics tortured people. This is the same place where people were unable to move around freely.

Today the place is breathing the air of freedom. We stepped into the main camp area and walked along the paved path into the building. The signs of occupation were scattered all over.

In the front building, there were a number of tables and chairs, all broken. The next room had a big refrigerator full of holes. The roof tiles and sheets were in pieces. The next room had many spring-beds and mattresses, all bloodstained.

We entered a huge room. The room was filled with food items; cheese tins, tinned milk, canned fish, milk powder, flour, rice, tea and many other kinds of food. I couldn't help but compare the frugal life of the pooralis and the military-soldier's life of comfort. There is, indeed, no comparison between a young poorali walking over stones and thorns in the forest and the army man enjoying a life of comfort.

Mounds of cigarette packets and butts were seen in many places. They were soaked in the rain and gave out an awful smell. Pornographic posters covered the walls. This is the camp of the Sri Lankan Army. How can one expect discipline from them? It appears that they actually prefer indiscipline. The kitchen walls were blackened with smoke. Rice, lentils and soy meat in three huge pots were sitting on the fireplace. They must have been cooked yesterday. The food had started to go off and was smelling bad. Master stirred the pots with the big wooden spoon and followed us.

The temple walls and the inn could be seen through the banana plantation. We quickly studied the police station and other buildings and went into the nuns' hostel. The walls were further protected on the inside with stacks of sandbags. Plenty of clothing soaked in blood lay all over.

'Come, let's go and see where the Black Tiger exploded.'

Both of us went ahead. In the ground, past the entrance to the main camp, close to its centre, was a massive crater. It told the story of Bork annai who made history in the blink of an eye. We stood silently for a moment.

Our motherland must rejoice for giving birth to souls who were ready to turn their lives into weapons to free her. The Tamil youth, those of Bork annai's age, must reflect on the nature of his love for the freedom of his homeland. Only when they do this will his dream be carried forward and fulfilled.

We again walked along the main road and arrived at Maankulam junction. We stood there and looked around.

'Master, look at the camp from here. How beautiful those big trees look. All this time this land was occupied and now it is ours.'

'How many more places there are like this. Look at the damage done by the bombers.'

As Master pointed, we saw the only remaining two-storeyed building. The shops near it were completely destroyed and the place looked like a graveyard. The railway station, too, looked distressing with its roof shattered.

'Come on. Let's look at the temple and the inn before we leave.'

We walked fast along the Mullaitheevu road. On one side, we saw the shops—all destroyed. On the other side were military posts and small houses. Then one side opened into vast paddy fields. On the other were the same symbols of occupation: sandbags all ripped apart.

The roadside had patches of blood here and there. They must be from our pooralis. These pooralis had stepped into the open space with only their bodies as cover.

As we looked at the open paddy fields, our hearts filled

with sorrow. Our pooralis had moved forward through this field. Oh, our Thileepan annai, Pirapa annai, Gopu and others would have lost their lives in this field.

'They are great souls,' said Master, his voice breaking with emotion.

'They gave us victory. Yet it is not easy to bear their loss.'

I changed the subject. 'Look at the temple and the inn. They have been completely destroyed.'

We walked past the inn and entered the temple. As I looked at the desecrated temple I had a strange feeling. When I was a child, this temple was the site of frequent caste clashes between people from some castes who wanted to enter and those who wanted to stop them from coming in. The latter insisted that allowing all castes to come would desecrate the temple environs. Now this same temple stood desecrated in the worst possible manner. None of the devotees who wanted to prevent other castes from entering the temple raised their voices against the worst form of desecration. Only the pooralis acted against it.

News that the enemy had withdrawn into the forest spread like wildfire among the people. They gathered around in groups, discussing it. Many civilians carrying their guns were out in the forest. We went and stayed in a village called Puthuvilaankulam. We stayed in five homes, in smaller groups. Master, Ithayan, Alahu, myself and six others stayed in the home of an old man.

We ate the lunch lovingly served to us and slept well.

We woke up only at 7.30 p.m. We drank the tea they brought us, and gathered in the front porch and sat with the old man as we waited for dinner. We have always enjoyed discussing issues with older folk and listening to their stories. I started the conversation.

'Have you been living here for long?'

'My father and mother started living in this area soon after they were married. They lived near the Nagathambiran temple in Puthur. I was born there. When I was about twenty years old, I got this forest land from the State and cleared it, after which I received the deed of ownership. When I got married I lived here; and my children were born here.'

'So how old are you now?'

'Maybe seventy-five. I was born in 1914, so you can work it out.'

'How many children do you have?'

'My eldest is a girl. She is living with her family in Kanakaraayankulam. The next was a boy. He was in some movement called PLOTE [People's Liberation Organisation of Tamil Eelam], and was shot and killed during the time the Indian Army was here. The last is my youngest boy. He has gone to the fields to spray the plants. He will be here any minute now.'

'Do you own a lot of land?' inquired Master.

'No, no. I have twenty-five acres. The paddy field and vegetable plots are all part of it. This house is also part of it. The coming of these low-caste fellows has ruined it all. I have now given it all up. Once a year I give a big feast to the people. That is all. Now all castes are earning money going overseas. Why should they respect people without much money like me?'

'All are humans. Why divide them by caste?' I said, interested in his reply.

'You cannot establish your caste status otherwise,' he replied. I realized it was pointless continuing on this topic with him.

'Iya, are you not going to send your youngest son overseas? They can earn a lot overseas,' Master asked him.

'Humph. Do you call that earning? There is so much fertile land in our homeland. There is plenty of water in the tanks. Why should you leave all this and go somewhere else? Neither my son nor I have considered it, even in our dreams. We can just eat kanchi and watch this forest, the land and the temple, and die here. I will never leave my land because of fear.'

One thing came out clearly in the discussion with the old man. He would support our armed freedom struggle in whatever way he could. He finds the idea of leaving the land and wasting its resources repulsive. He stands firm on this. Yet, he is not able to give up some of his traditional views on society. This is where the younger generation needs to change. The younger generation today has the responsibility to guide their parents. Even if a few of them are unable to change, the young ones must change in readiness for our new nation.

Look at the community in China. If one million students demonstrated in Tiananmen Square demanding democratic rights, they certainly did not do so with the permission of their parents. If these students can organize such a massive protest, why cannot the younger generation here, with the help of pooralis, take up progressive action to change society? When the entire Tamil nation under a single leadership steps out with one goal, that day of freedom will be commemorated as our fallen heroes' day. Before we reach that point, let us destroy the backward ideas in society and develop our human and natural resources to improve our economic status.

'Iya, tell us about your fields and your horticulture.'

'It is the same as talking about my life.'

'Good, we can learn about both at the same time,' I encouraged him.

'Wait, thambi. This boy has misplaced my tobacco leaves,' he said and went inside his humble mud cottage.

A young man walked in from outside, gave us a friendly smile and went in, calling out, 'Appa.'

'Where did you put my tobacco leaves, boy?'

A little later the old man came out and sat down with a home-rolled cigar in his mouth.

'Like the cigar?' asked Master.

'Oh! Do you really . . . ?' said the old man in a warning tone because pooralis are not permitted to smoke. But he was happy to have two sets of ears willing to listen to his old stories.

'When I was about twenty or twenty-five, a white man came and expanded and renovated this tank. It used to hold a lot of water then. They said that if anyone was willing to clear the forest and cultivate it for five years they would give him the ownership deed for the land. None of our people were willing.'

'Why not? It is fertile land, isn't it?'

'You can say that now. Then it was the domain of elephants. There were very few people around here. Even the white man would not come without his gun.'

'Then how could you . . . ?'

'Wait,' said the old man, as he puffed on his cigar.

'My mother and father were adamant that I should not do it. But I was keen. I went to the white man and somehow managed to get hold of a gun. My father was hopping mad when he found out. He shouted saying I had no right to bring a gun inside the house. I was persistent. I found a piece of forest land that would get plenty of water and cleared the forest. Every year the crop would do well, but when it was nearly ready the animals would come and destroy it all.'

'Did you not get fed up?'

'No, I persisted. I cultivated the land every year and slowly started to save some money. Then I got married.' He puffed on his cigar. 'It was only later that other people came. They were all emboldened by my presence.'

We were all enjoying the old man's tales flattering himself.

'One night—my hut was then located on that raised bit of land there—Velan, my neighbour, came running and screaming. He said four or five elephants had come into his fields and they were refusing to move despite his gunfire. He pleaded with me to come.

'I cursed him because of the bother, but I went. There were several elephants. I was slightly drunk. I could not see well. An elephant blew hard and the gust threw me back.

I landed on my hand and dislocated it. When I turned to look, five or six pairs of eyes were staring at me. I was not steady enough to run. I fired with one hand, all the while lying on the ground. All the elephants started running. The next day people said that they had found a dead elephant lying in the forest. White men and Sinhalese came and shook my hand. Those were the days.'

'So you are a great hunter?'

'Of course. If I shoot, I never miss. I was a great hunter. Later there were children and now I live like this.'

As the old man puffed at his cigar, we suddenly heard continuous gunfire. We quickly readied ourselves, put some of the pooralis on guard around the cannon and left with fifteen pooralis on a tractor. We made contact through the walkie-talkie and parked the tractor one kilometre from the location of the fire and started to run in formation.

We learnt that the clashes were taking place under the command of Maathavan annai.

We were about to proceed in the dark from Puthuvilaankulam into the forest in the wrong direction when a voice from behind stopped us.

'Wait. I will also come with you. Where do you want to go? Tell me.'

Only when he came very close did I realize that he was the youngest son of the old man. He was holding a hunting gun.

'Oh, it is you,' he said. 'You were all at the teacher's house. You all left suddenly without telling me. I came running with the gun and ten cartridges without even putting on a shirt. Where should we go?'

We told him the spot and the direction in which we were to attack. He led us, saying he would show us the way.

As I followed him, others came behind us in formation. We were struggling to keep up with him. He was walking very fast, at the same time making way by clearing tree branches and bushes. We were compelled to run to keep up with him. He stopped for a moment and pulled something from his foot and continued walking.

'Annai, did you come without even wearing sandals?' I asked.

'Oh, we are used to it,' he said.

He kept his gun above his head while walking and moved it constantly to avoid bushes and branches. When we reached the spot I told the pooralis to take position and then asked Maathavan on the walkie-talkie for a rundown of the situation. He described the strengths and weaknesses of the enemy's situation at that moment. I gave orders to the pooralis and we advanced through the darkness.

Suddenly dark clouds gathered, and within a few seconds there was strong wind and heavy rain. The noise prevented us from accurately gauging the situation. Even though we were now walking along the railway track we had trouble seeing anything.

Despite the setback caused by the heavy rain, we walked fast and continued through to Kanakaraayankulam junction. As we reached the junction the rain had eased somewhat. People had gathered outside in large numbers. News and rumours about the military escaping into the forest were spreading quickly among the people.

The majority of the men among them were carrying hunting guns and shotguns. Suddenly there was some excitement. People were gathering around two men who had just arrived on a bicycle. The two men were talking loudly. People were firing questions at them. One man started telling what had happened. 'You know the surroundings of the Kanakaraayankulam fields, the open space. A girl who stepped outside her home was shot by three army men who were hiding there.'

'Is she dead?'

'No, no, the bullet hit her leg. We all chased the army fellows when we heard the gunfire. They tried to hide in the bushes. We surrounded the area and shot into it twice. They came out with raised hands, saying in Sinhalese that they were surrendering. Arasu annai spoke to them. But our people were careless. They were not alert and the three ran away after pushing over the two people who were watching them.'

'Oh no! You should have been more careful,' said a man.

Most of the people listening to the story were very disappointed. They were also discussing another story of a woman who captured two army men hiding under a bridge. We walked along with a smile on our face.

'Master, what do you think of our people?' I asked.

'Looks as if they will beat the hell out of them if they get the chance,' laughed Master.

'What else do you expect? What do we know about what these people were put through by the army for years?' I said.

An old man with a cigar in his mouth and a shotgun over his shoulder cycled past.

'Now the people come out and talk excitedly after we have chased the army from the camp. Why didn't they come out sooner and join us in the battle?' I asked.

'Only now do people have the determination to get rid of the Maankulam camp. Times are changing. If this attitude continues, it will be great,' replied Master.

It was now 6.15 p.m. We had forgotten about lunch.

A man coming fast towards us on a bicycle suddenly applied the brakes and stopped a few metres past us.

'Thambi, thambi,' he called urgently, and we ran to him.

'There is a shop at the turn there. I saw a man there running into the house near it. I heard a woman screaming and also someone talking in Sinhalese. It must be the army. People are saying that some army men were seen around here in the afternoon.'

'We must get at least one of them. Run fast,' Master shouted at the top of his voice.

As we neared the house, we broke up into two groups. We made one group surround the area in a wide circle to stop anyone trying to escape. The other group moved forward towards the house. When we neared the house and took our position we heard some talking. We could hear some Sinhala conversation in between. Once we surrounded the house, I hid behind a flowering bush and listened carefully.

'Our father gave you all the dowry you deserved. How dare you come now to our father's funeral and demand the thaali around our mother's neck,' shouted a male voice.

Another male voice spoke in broken Tamil with a Sinhala accent. 'She was wrong to ask for it, brother-in-law. Please do not be angry.'

'Who are you to touch me, you Sinhala bastard. Let go of me,' the first man shouted in a drunken voice.

A woman was cursing at the top of her voice.

I signalled the rest and we withdrew quietly from the scene.

Master, with his gun in ready position, queried, 'What happened? Couldn't you catch anyone?'

We gathered everyone hiding in readiness behind the bushes and told them what was going on in the house.

We all had a good laugh. But they were all mildly annoyed that their time had been wasted like this.

We continued with our move. It was getting dark and we moved cautiously. Monkeys and other animals suddenly jumped in front of us, delaying our journey.

When we reached Puthuvilaankulam it was 9.45 p.m. We had not eaten anything since morning. People gave us idiyappam and meat curry. We rested after the meal.

26 November 1990

At 9 a.m. we stationed one group to keep watch and the rest went to the lake for a bath.

As we had already planned, we divided ourselves into two groups and entered the lake. We spent more time having water fights than bathing, and made a huge racket. We got out and dried ourselves. I had just finished putting on my clean dry clothes when I suddenly found myself in the lake again. Master and Alahu, standing with their hands on their hips, were laughing.

After lunch we went to the forest and picked some wood apples and made a spicy mixture with coconut and chillies. We had a competition to see who could eat the most.

We chatted with the people. They all seemed very excited. One man said, 'Tomorrow Balraj annai is going to raise the Tiger flag in Maankulam camp. Today you can all sleep happily.'

We all slept well.

27 November 1990

We started early the next morning, on two tractors, towards the Maankulam camp. This camp that had flown the flag of occupation, and from which untold brutalities had been committed, today appeared totally destroyed.

O, maaveerars! You stood with us shoulder to shoulder and shared our burdens. You entered the minds and bodies and indeed, every cell of the enemy, and petrified them. You bravely entered open fields to destroy the enemy hiding in his camp. Knowing well that your life would end in a few seconds you turned your bodies into weapons, as Black Tigers. You move in a grand procession in the breeze that embraces Maankulam.

The maaveerar meet at the gentle running waters. They smile in the soft noises made by forest trees. They come down as raindrops and kiss this land. They come with the soft rays of the moon to embrace us. They enter our hearts through the dancing peacocks and the songs of the mynah.

This land soaked in their blood will be enriched.

They are the guards of our borders. They will be born again and again through Mother Tamil. The sun will no longer burn us. In the movement of their lips, in the words they speak, in their eyes, the pooralis will keep the maaveerars alive. For the freedom that will come, they will train the new generation.

They are the suns that never set.

The villages, paddy fields and lanes in which they played will never forget them.

They are the life behind all of nature's actions.

As we drove away, we watched the destroyed camp for a final moment before it disappeared behind us.

As our tractors with the cannons moved towards Jaffna town, we turned backed and waved. Tears filled our eyes.

The white clouds in the blue sky moved in the opposite direction.

The buildings of Kokkaavil started to appear in the distance. A soft voice sang in my ears.

The clouds in the sky will sing.

They will utter the names of the maaveerars.

Rivers of tears will flow from our eyes.

Here end my memories of the Maankulam attack. My heart is already starting to fill with the memories of the Silaavathurai attack.

Before Malaravan could start writing about his experience in the Silaavathurai attack he became a maaveerar on 23 November 1992 during the attack on the Palaly Camp East.

A Man of Deeds

The following are memories of Malaravan written in 1993 by the late S.P. Tamilselvan (Head of the Political Wing of the LTTE).

'O, my dearest Malaravan, my heart is filled with anxiety because of my inability to write about your life, which, if written by a good writer, will turn into a great epic. I am saddened, my friend, that I cannot do justice to that great life of yours. Yet I do desire to share the great memories of the time I spent with you, which I recall often.

'I met you first in 1991, when I took up my responsibility as the Head of the Political Wing for Jaffna district. I came to meet the Paseelan Mortar Unit, and at that time you were a group leader within that unit. You got up and said to me, "Our division size has been reduced. Many have died or been seriously injured. If we are given new people we can train them and make our division even stronger than what it is now." I detected, then, your intelligence, dedication and eagerness.

'It is appropriate to describe the Paseelan Mortar Unit before I continue with your story. At the mention of the name Paseelan, the enemy will start looking for an escape route. Such was the challenge posed by our Paseelan mortars. They are equal to the mortars of developed countries. Indeed, joining the Paseelan Mortar Unit is not an easy path. Many will hesitate because of the rigorous training required. Yet, the fighters in our Paseelan Unit trained themselves with dedication and made it into what it is now. This mortar division had played important roles in many of our great battle victories. Malaravan, you are among the tireless fighters of this Paseelan Mortar Unit.'

I have never seen Malaravan taking a break from work. He would always be doing something. He would be either estimating the speed and reach of the mortars or cleaning his mortar. At other times he would be giving classes to his fellow fighters explaining various aspects of the unit. Our fighters were making history at that time. Many of the enemy camps were destroyed and our national flag was raised. Malaravan's contribution was notable in each of these victories.

In Malaravan, I saw the traits of courage and tact, combined with hard training, which our leader [LTTE leader Pirapaaharan] would often list as desirable traits in a fighter. I also saw the trait of leadership in Malaravan. Within a short time he had gained the ability to plan which is an essential for a leader of a fighting unit. He is not a man of many words. His actions compensate for his lack of words. This is a characteristic to be found in our leader too. At times this trait in Malaravan would be displayed in another form. I have watched in amazement as Malaravan started to explain things, using words which would come clear and crisp. I also saw another talent in Malaravan. He was a kind and capable teacher to his fellow fighters whom he treated with great affection. Many of his comrades have also confirmed this to me.

'O Malaravan, I will recollect some of my memories of you. Many locations such as Maankulam, Manalaaru, Mullaitheevu, Jaffna Fort and Palaly crop up, urging me to tell your stories. Your agonies in Silaavathurai, your recovery from near death, your playfulness in the face of danger, pain and misery, your tenacity that transformed these into achievements: it is these qualities that we admire in you. You took your mortar in front of the enemy camp without any cover and fired non-stop. I can still picture that scene. Watching you, I never believed that you would come back alive. The enemy fire had damaged the vehicle carrying your mortar. But you carried on with tact and courage. The sight of you bringing back your mortar safely, without any concern for your own life, is still fresh in my mind.

'O Malaravan, when we began our journey for the Silaavathurai attack, our regiments started moving at night to avoid detection. It was a dense forest, but a road ran beside it. We struggled to move the Paseelan Mortar Regiment. You and your fellow fighters would move all night with your mortar. Despite all our efforts we could only move it for a limited distance each night. We had to travel through that path many times for various needs and we were constantly concerned that our movements might be detected by the enemy. During the day you would hide in the forest camouflaging everything and everyone. Then you and your fellow fighters would cook in a pot by the road, and eat, sleep and enjoy yourselves. Watching you, I too felt like joining your group. Those capable fighters like you successfully completed the task.

'Yes, Malaravan, your approach to dangers and difficulties and also your disposition to make everyone happy and enthusiastic made you an ideal fighter. Even now, when I reflect on your dangerous and challenging battlefront actions, I am surprised that you came back alive after the Karainagar battle. When the decision was made after this battle to temporarily halt the operations of the Paseelan Unit, even I was shaken by your outrage at this decision. Later when you were given the explanation for the decision you accepted it with sadness and cooperated.

'Malaravan, I have only mentioned a few of your achievements on the battlefront. Later, when I said to you, "Presently there are only a very few experienced people in the political division. You must work in this field for some time," you accepted it. You always had the fighter's disposition to accept your leader's requests wholeheartedly. You were thus made the leader of the student division for Jaffna district.

'It was only during this phase that I learnt of your achievements as a student and about your family background. Your father is a doctor. Your mother is also a talented person. I learnt that your brothers are doctors and graduates. You, who excelled academically, were the best student among them all. I heard that even while reading Grade 9 you sat for the GCE examinations and, to the amazement of everyone, passed with distinctions in more than half the subjects. Later you received distinctions in all subjects and were selected as the top student in the school. You obtained all-island-top marks in Tamil.

'Malaravan, your whole family is connected with our struggle. Your brother is a doctor and he too is a fighter. Your father, even in his old age, has dedicated his life to serve the people of Vanni who were struggling with very few facilities. One can see him even near battle lines, serving the injured.'

It was during this period that we felt the need for experts to develop some of the sectors. As requested by our leader we made arrangements for some of the fighters who had joined us after obtaining university admission to continue their education at the university. Some of them stubbornly refused to take up studies and insisted that they had joined the movement to fight and not study. Our leader spoke to them and convinced them to continue their studies. Our leader told them, 'You do not have to study for yourself or to assist your life. You must study for this struggle, to help the movement.' Knowing Malaravan's abilities I too asked Malaravan to continue his studies. But I did not force him. His exceptional qualities had created in me a respect for him. I never had to order him. Before I could tell him he would understand my thoughts and put them into action. When I asked him to study he stood silently, looking at the ground. I said, 'Malaravan, do take time to think about it and then decide.' I think that though he had the desire to study, something within him stopped him from doing so. Many of his fellow fighters—with whom he joked, laughed, ate, had fun and fought bravely together with at battlefronts—are no more. Perhaps it was their memories that prevented him from taking up studies. I have seen tears in his eyes and heard his voice break whenever their names came up in conversations.

'Malaravan, one fellow fighter with whom you spent a long time and with whom you fought many battles was Major Lamba. He was in charge of the Paseelan Mortar Unit. He was killed in 1992 in the Palavegaya-2 military operation to recapture Elephant Pass from us. You were with me at that time. That was a cruel day. I understood your heart that day. You stood outraged even in the face of that tragedy. You demanded that Lamba's weapon be given to you. You somehow got your request and obtained his weapon. Then I did not see you that whole night. The battle was raging. I thought you had returned to the battlefront and I went away. When I arrived the next morning you stood in front of me with a few sheets of paper in your hand. You gave them to me and said, "I have written about Lamba. I am going back to the battle." You instructed me to send your write-up about Lamba to the paper.

'Even in the middle of that intense battle while artillery and bullets whizzed past close to us, in the middle of that night, in some corner, in a tiny light, you wrote that piece thinking of Lamba. When I read it tears welled up in my eyes. I then understood your haste in writing that piece. I also understood your urge to obtain Lamba's weapon. But I did not show this to you. At times your actions indicated that in the grip of emotion and outrage you could lose your cool and put yourself in unnecessary danger in the battles. I therefore decided not to send you to the battlefront till you calmed down. Without letting you know my thoughts, I kept you behind lines with other tasks. Only on that day did I see your hatred and anger towards me. Yet, we the children of our leader, followed his training for discipline, courage, perseverance and obedience. You too followed this and carried out your tasks.

'After this, we were collating the battle details from fighters who were at various battlefronts. Then you would comment that if we had planned it this way or operated that way we could have won or reduced our losses. You would thus demonstrate your intelligence, your leadership qualities and your abilities in planning. You were most definitely growing up to be a leader in our liberation journey. That hope and dream came to a tragic end. O Malaravan, we have not allowed our loss to make us hesitant. Even in your absence you gave us the determination to reach our goal. We could keep on writing about you. Days are not enough.

'Malaravan, when I am writing about you, your family often comes in my thoughts. When we were battling on one battlefront, your brother would be treating the injured fighters, giving back their lives to our dearest brothers, at another front. Even your father would join in. Your mother and other brothers would fast for the battle victory. There is no need to say anything else about your family.

'Malaravan, that last day, the day we lost you, the day you departed, I can never forget that day. Though we were all energetic and enthusiastic when the battle started, we were also very tired because we had laboured many days and nights for this attack. If by some error the enemy was alerted about our planned attack, many of our brothers would lose their lives. Our leader had repeatedly mentioned this during the preparations for the attack and everyone's mind was troubled by this possibility. When our battle leader, Balraj, gave us orders to move towards the battle line, we did so with trepidation. The thoughts and worries that passed through our minds in those few hours cannot be put down in words. Then we heard the news that the main division had reached its position. The joy that filled our hearts then, we could never experience again in our lives. For an instant you lost your cool and jumped up and down and rolled on the ground to express your joy of victory. I cannot forget that sight.

'The attack started and the battle was raging. We were receiving news of victories from various fronts. Captured weapons were piling up. Since our position was not very safe, the captured weapons had to be moved away immediately. I looked for you to give you that responsibility. I was angry when others nearby told me that you had gone to the front line. A little later, I saw you carrying a heavy load of captured weapons and walking towards our camp struggling for breath. I opened my mouth to scold you, but I couldn't. Later I called you and instructed you not to go far away from me. You then undertook the responsibility of moving the weapons.

'During the last phase of that battle, artillery was exploding all around us like rain. This proved to us our victory in the battle. The enemy had either died or run away from the front lines. That is why there was ceaseless firing from their back lines. That was why he was raining artillery inside his own area. We continued with our tasks even in the middle of the artillery fire because we had to clear all the captured weapons, the injured fighters and the bodies of our dead comrades before daylight. Like the farmers who work in the rain, our fighters were doing their task in artillery rain. Joyous about our victory we were sending the expensive captured military equipment, when . . .'

That tragedy, that unthinkable event happened. Three artillery shells came whizzing and exploded in front of us. It took away three of our friends. Everyone there, except one, was seriously injured. Among them was Malaravan.

We sent everyone to the treatment location. A person standing near me told me that Malaravan's injury was serious and that his leg had been severed. I kept telling myself that it did not matter if he lost his leg, that he would still achieve many great things. I hoped and hoped that he would live. Among the many hundreds of fighters, a few, even in such conditions, will demonstrate extraordinary abilities. Malaravan was among those few.

'At this same time, your brother, at the medical line behind us, was treating the injured. He was so very fond of you. But as we all returned at the end of the battle we heard that shocking news—the news that crushed our hearts.'

Malaravan died on his way to the hospital. . . .

'Everyone's face was covered in tears. I heard that your brother sobbed uncontrollably on hearing the news. Yes, he too has seen many bodies of dead comrades and experienced the cost of freedom. He tried to console himself by putting you among them.

'Yes, Malaravan, your life of struggle and your actions will not only be a guide to us all, yours will be an exemplary life in our brave and determined liberation struggle. Malaravan, we are learning more about your abilities even after you have departed. This book is just one among them. There is no doubt that this book will register deeply in the hearts of our future generations.

'Three days after your final event, I went to your home with hesitation. I imagined the situation that would prevail in many homes under such circumstance. But your family's reaction was something I could never have imagined, something that was completely out of the ordinary. Everyone at your home was crying. When they saw us they wiped their tears and welcomed us. Suddenly your brother went inside, brought some papers and gave them to your father. Your father gave them to me and requested that one be given to the Senchcholai Children's Home and the other be used for the expenses to treat injured fighters. I opened it. Yes, they were two bank accounts in the name of Malaravan. There were hundreds of thousands of rupees in them. It was the money your father had banked for you since your birth. The money had grown manifoldly. I understood then that your uniqueness was also to be found in your family.'

Reminiscences of a Mother

Our family is from Jaffna. The place hardly needs introduction because Tamils from Jaffna are today spread across the world. About ten kilometres from Jaffna city stands the village of Sandilippaay. This beautiful village is famous for the Seerani Naagammaal temple: a temple for the mother goddess. Malaravan was born in this village on 8 April 1972 as the fourth and youngest son to Kaasilingam (my husband) and myself (Atputharaani).

Malaravan was named Vijinthan by our family. The eldest of his three brothers, Sujanthan, is a medical doctor. The next one, Jeyanthan, is a teacher. The third brother, Rejinthan, is also a medical doctor. Malaravan's father too is a medical doctor who served his patients with total dedication. Malaravan grew up in our family with an abundance of love and care. His parents, brothers, grandparents and uncles: all of us adored him. His playmates included not only the neighbourhood children but also his older brothers. At the age of three Malaravan would play marbles as an equal with his older brothers and even beat them because he could aim and hit the marbles accurately.

His brothers would be amazed at his daring and intelligence which was far beyond his age.

Malaravan loved spending time with older folks. He would be eager to find out about their youth and the games they played as children. He would simply smile when they exaggerated the antics of their younger days. Later on Malaravan would make satirical comments about these, to embarrass them. The older folks too enjoyed talking to Malaravan. He was full of questions as they narrated their experiences. Yet, they never got annoyed and always patted him on his head for his curiosity. Malaravan would embellish the stories he heard from the older folks and repeat them to his friends in a highly animated manner. His friends would be mesmerized. He loved punning. Sometimes his friends, not catching on, would get angry. Once Malaravan made them realize what he meant they would all laugh together.

Whenever Malaravan was with his friends there would be loud laughter and joy. It was easy to know where he was just by this. Often he did not have to go over to his friends' places to play—they would come to our house. Malaravan would introduce new games to them or make changes to old games. Sometimes when they played hide-and-seek he would hide behind a tree. He would go round and round the tree with agility and speed, making it hard for his friends to catch him. When they felt annoyed by this, he would tell a traditional humorous story based on Tenali Raman and they would all break into loud laughter.

He loved animals. There were two dogs at our home. Malaravan would share with them the biscuits and other snacks given to him. He would toss the food in the air and enjoy watching them jump up to catch it. When he had to go out at night he would take both dogs with him. Once, while they were walking, a snake came slithering very near Malaravan's feet. One of the dogs tugged at Malaravan's shorts and dragged him away, while the other attacked and killed the snake. Malaravan became even more attached to the dogs after this incident.

He loved the goats, cows and hens that were reared at home. He would stroke the calf and feed it grass with his hand. Watching him it was obvious that he was one with the calf—lost in that experience. He named the goat kid Mani. It would come running at his call. He loved baby chickens. He would let them out of their basket and enjoy watching them running around. He would pick them up one at a time, and stroke them. He had names for each one of them. The chickens too would collect around his feet the moment they heard his voice. They would even jump on his shoulders and head. A love for living things was deeply ingrained in him.

He started school at the age of five at Sandilippaay Hindu College. A diligent student, he kept all his pranks for outside the classroom. He was never a nuisance in class though he asked a lot of questions to the teachers. He studied easily. One did not need to push him to work at his lessons. He always came first and won prizes in all the subjects.

Once he started school he became an avid reader. At the age of seven he was reading picture-storybooks. He quickly went on to read short-story collections. He began reading full-length novels at the age of nine. His favourite writer was Chandilyan[1]. He absorbed Chandilyan's style of

---

[1]Chandilyan was and still is a very popular Tamil author of historical novels.

describing scenes from nature. People around Malaravan were astonished to see him reading big books that were too heavy for him to carry. Once he started on a book he forgot the world around him and became one with its characters. If his back began to hurt he would lie down on the spot and continue reading. No one could distract him. He would forget food and sleep. When he came out of the book, his eyes would be swollen and red. People would teasingly call him a bookworm; that never bothered him. He would even pick out papers from the waste bin that had writing on them, and put away some of them if they contained good things that might come in handy later on.

In his younger days he prayed regularly. He went to the temple every Friday with his grandmother. He would distribute the food given by the priest to the devotees at the temple. He enjoyed volunteering at the temple. He loved celebrating festival days. He found immense pleasure spring-cleaning the house, making festival foods and sharing it with neighbours, and lighting firecrackers. He would assist me with all the chores in preparation for festivals. He would cry and demand that his father, brothers, grandfather, uncles, and I, all buy firecrackers for him. After lighting some of them he would save the rest. He never wasted anything and put limits on everything he did and everything he used, including food, clothing and the like.

He would help me in the kitchen. He enjoyed cutting vegetables and making tea and cool drinks. When he and his brothers were tired after play, his brothers would urge him to make something cool to drink, buttering him up with compliments like, 'You are the best cool-drink maker. Please make us some too.' He would angrily retort, 'Am I your servant to do all this?', and walk away. A little later he would come out with a trayful of cool drinks for everyone. Enjoying them, the brothers would attempt to praise Malaravan, to which he would respond with, 'You are all lazy donkeys.' It was a joy to watch the scene.

Malaravan completed his fifth year of schooling at Sandilippaay Hindu College. Around this time his father was transferred to Mullaitheevu Hospital. The family moved to the village of Mulliyavalai in that district. Malaravan continued his schooling at Mulliyavalai Viththiyaananthaa College. Two of Malaravan's brothers got into Jaffna University. The family without the father—the four sons and I—moved back to Jaffna, near Jaffna University. Malaravan continued his schooling at St John's College in Jaffna. He completed his GCE Ordinary Level examination with straight As. He continued his studies for the University entrance examination. As his parents we had very high hopes for Malaravan, more so than for his brothers. Such were also the expectations held by most people who knew him.

Malaravan was very organized. He would set his alarm clock for 4 a.m., wrapping the clock in cloth so that the sound of the alarm did not disturb the others in the house. At 6 a.m. he would stop studying and feed the colourful fish in his fish tank, a present given to him by his second-eldest brother. He would sit beside the tank, engrossed in watching the fish feed. He would then come out into the front yard. The buds in the garden would be ready to open. He would observe each plant and caress the flowers. He did not like to pick them, believing that flowers should be enjoyed on the plant. Perhaps it is because of his love of flowers that he changed the name given to him by the LTTE, Leo, to Malaravan[2]. He would then

---

[2]Malaravan is the conjuction of two words: malar (flower) and avan (he), which translates to 'He, the flower'.

go to the vegetable plot in the backyard and examine each plant on which a vegetable was growing. In the evening he would water the nursery plants. During the holidays he would manure the garden and plant some seedlings or saplings. Sharp at 7.30 a.m. he would take a bath, have breakfast, put on his uniform and go off to school. I would watch him disappear in the distance on his motorbike. I would imagine that a white pigeon was flying off into the sky. Dreams about his future filled my thoughts.

Barely had he entered the house after coming back from school, that he would call out to me to ask whether I had fed his fish. I would bring a cup of tea for him, but he would have disappeared into the backyard to water the nursery plants. I would take the tea to the backyard. Malaravan would reprimand me gently for bringing the tea out there. He would say he was saddened to see the plants drooping under the hot sun and that he had to water them. I understood my son's feelings and returned to the house with the empty cup.

Often on my shopping trips I would buy his favourite fruits. Malaravan would hint that he would have preferred a book instead. When I brought out the book I had hidden, his face would brighten. I enjoyed watching this sight. For festivals I would purchase clothes for all my four sons. The older brothers would wait for Malaravan to choose first.

In 1990 the Lankan military besieged at the Dutch Fort in Jaffna tried to get out. There were frequent aerial bombings and artillery fire. The Elephant-Pass route connecting Jaffna to the rest of the island was closed and many essential items became hard to get. The poor were struggling for food. Jaffna's teaching-hospital was closed. Shops in town also closed.

Schools were closed indefinitely. Malaravan felt frustrated by the interruptions to his studies. He began examining the reasons for this situation. He came to the decision that at least future generations must enjoy freedom.

The result of this decision was that our joyful home lost its joy. Our family could not object to his considered and reasonable decision. Following military training and some battles he came home for a week's holiday, following the Maankulam battle. There was joy in the home again. Laughter was heard again. I had made him a shirt in his favourite green colour. He asked for the symbol of the student division to be stitched on it. I obliged. He came home again a few months later and said he had been made the coordinator of the Jaffna student division. He would be wearing that green shirt most of the time. I was overjoyed to see how fond he was of it.

During the short time he was in the student section he achieved many things and launched many projects. He discussed his plans with teachers and university professors, and carried out many of them. They were amazed at Malaravan's enthusiasm for education. He collected statistics on the shortages in the resources of Jaffna schools and investigated ways to overcome them. Though many are unaware of his services at this time, no one can deny his love for education. His duties changed again in a few months. This time it was to write reports on important events. He worked hard, day and night. During this phase he met with a motorbike accident and temporarily lost the use of his left arm. He began writing profusely; because he was writing continuously he suffered from severe backache. He bought and took painkillers, and continued his writing.

Malaravan brought home all his writing. He gave it to me and asked for comments. I had stitched him another green shirt. He asked for a picture to be embroidered on it. When I asked what he wanted, he pointed to the picture of a poorali carrying a maaveeran. On his next visit home, I gave him a shirt embroidered with the picture. He put it on and admired himself in the mirror. He praised me for the beautiful work. When he bid us goodbye that time it was drizzling. Everyone at home went to the door and watched him leave. He did look handsome in that shirt. I watched him till he disappeared in the distance. None of us knew then that it would be our last meeting.

The news that Malaravan had become a maaveerar came a week later. His body was placed in the hall. His two dogs jumped on the coffin, licking his cheeks. Everyone was touched seeing the dogs' love for him. His father was in Mullaitheevu. All the routes were closed and it took three days for him to come home by sea. On the last day his two dogs tried to prevent those carrying his coffin from leaving the house by holding their legs tight. It was with great difficulty that the dogs were restrained. Malaravan, oblivious to the goings-on, began his last journey with a smile on his face.

This maaveerar who lived by the motto: 'My body to my land, and my soul to Tamil' made his short, twenty years of life meaningful, and continues to live among us through his writing.

Atputharaani
2012

Glossary

aachchi: grandmother; a generic term also used, in Tamil culture, for someone old enough to be a grandmother.

acca: refers to elder sister; a generic term also used, in Tamil culture, to address anyone old enough to be an elder sister.

alkaaddi: a bird that nests on the ground and lets out a scream when animals or humans threaten its eggs. Its scream usually gives away the movement of people and therefore is useful during battles. The term literally means 'giving away the whereabouts of people'.

amma: used in the same sense as the word 'mum' in English. However, in Tamil culture, it is also used to refer to any woman who is old enough to be a mother.

appa: used in the same sense as the word 'dad'.

anna(i): refers to elder brother; also a generic term to address anyone old enough to be an elder brother.

baila: popular form of song and dance among Sinhala people.

Black Tiger: poorali who is a member of the LTTE suicide squad.

iya: used in a similar sense as 'sir'.

kanchi: poor man's diet of rice gruel.

maaveerar: poorali(s) killed in confrontation with the enemy. The people of Tamil Eelam commemorate Maaveerar Day on 27 November.

machan: a form of address between male friends; used in the same sense as 'mate' in English.

naaval: large tree that bears tiny purple plums.

naayuruvi: common bush plant.

neem: common tree found in homes.

poorali: (plural—pooralis) someone waging a struggle against injustice; commonly used today by the Tamil community in the island to refer to members of the LTTE.

paalai: common forest tree in the area.

poovarasu: common tree planted along fences around homes.

tank: (also called lake) natural rainwater catchment improved to retain water for irrigation. Used since ancient times, they are a common form of irrigation in this part of the world.

thaali: the thick gold chain that is put on the bride's neck by the groom. A symbol of marriage, it is removed by the wife when the husband dies.

thambi: refers to younger brother; a generic term also used in Tamil culture to address anyone young enough to be a younger brother.

thaaththaa: grandfather; a generic term also used in Tamil culture for someone old enough to be a grandfather.

thula: a form of irrigation that works by drawing water from wells. The thula is the long trunk of the palmyra tree fitted with a hinge in the middle. A person walks on the trunk to lower the bucket into the well, and then walks back the same way to lift the bucket filled with water.

veera: common forest tree found in the area

water canal: canals dug out along roads to carry the water from the tanks to the paddy fields. The water supply is controlled by sluice gates.